Alec Butler

Canada's Two-Spirit LGBTQ Voice – Unfiltered

Rajesh Gonzalez

ISBN: 9781779696939
Imprint: Telephasic Workshop
Copyright © 2024 Rajesh Gonzalez.
All Rights Reserved.

Contents

Introduction

The rise of Alec Butler

Alec's early life in rural Canada

Alec Butler was born in a small rural town in Canada, a place characterized by its breathtaking landscapes and tight-knit community. However, beneath the picturesque exterior lay the complexities of growing up in an environment that often struggled to embrace diversity. Alec's early life was marked by a series of experiences that would shape their identity and fuel their passion for activism.

From a young age, Alec felt different from their peers. In a society that often equated masculinity with strength and femininity with fragility, Alec's fluidity in gender expression was a source of confusion and conflict. The traditional gender roles prevalent in rural Canada posed a significant challenge, as Alec navigated the expectations placed upon them by family, friends, and society at large. This struggle is encapsulated in Judith Butler's theory of gender performativity, which suggests that gender is not an inherent quality but rather a series of actions and performances shaped by societal norms. Alec's journey was one of resisting and redefining these norms, often feeling like a misfit in a world that demanded conformity.

Alec's family, while loving, adhered to conventional values that often clashed with Alec's emerging identity. The concept of Two-Spirit identity, rooted in Indigenous cultures, was foreign to them, yet it resonated deeply with Alec's sense of self. The term "Two-Spirit" is used by some Indigenous peoples to describe a person who embodies both masculine and feminine spirits, a concept that challenges the binary understanding of gender. Alec's exploration of this identity became a beacon of hope, guiding them through the tumultuous waters of adolescence.

As a teenager, Alec began to express their feelings through art. Drawing, painting, and writing became outlets for their emotions, allowing them to

1

communicate their struggles and triumphs in ways that words alone could not capture. This artistic expression was not merely a hobby; it was a lifeline. The act of creating became a form of resistance against the limitations imposed by their environment. As they delved deeper into the world of art, Alec discovered the works of LGBTQ artists who had paved the way for voices like theirs. Artists such as Keith Haring and Frida Kahlo served as inspirations, demonstrating that art could be a powerful tool for advocacy and change.

The isolation of rural life often compounded the challenges Alec faced. With few resources and limited access to LGBTQ support networks, Alec turned to the internet as a means of connection. Online communities provided a safe space to explore their identity, share experiences, and find solidarity with others who understood the nuances of being LGBTQ in a conservative setting. This digital refuge was crucial in fostering a sense of belonging that was often absent in their immediate surroundings.

Despite the hardships, Alec's early life was also marked by moments of joy and discovery. The beauty of the Canadian wilderness offered solace and inspiration. Alec often found themselves wandering through the forests and fields, drawing strength from the natural world. This connection to nature would later influence their artistic endeavors, as they sought to capture the essence of their experiences through vibrant colors and evocative imagery.

However, the journey was not without its difficulties. The pervasive homophobia and transphobia in Alec's community manifested in both subtle and overt ways. Bullying and discrimination were part of daily life, and the fear of rejection loomed large. The psychological toll of these experiences cannot be overstated; studies show that LGBTQ youth are at a higher risk for mental health issues, including depression and anxiety, often stemming from societal rejection and lack of support. Alec's resilience in the face of such adversity was a testament to their strength, but it also highlighted the urgent need for change within their community.

As Alec transitioned into adulthood, the desire to break free from the constraints of rural life grew stronger. The decision to move to the city was both liberating and daunting. It represented a leap into the unknown, but also a chance to find community and acceptance. The urban landscape promised a vibrant LGBTQ scene, filled with opportunities for connection, expression, and activism. This pivotal moment marked the beginning of Alec's journey as a vocal advocate for LGBTQ rights, setting the stage for the impactful work they would undertake in the years to come.

In summary, Alec Butler's early life in rural Canada was a complex tapestry woven with threads of struggle, creativity, and resilience. The challenges they faced in a conservative environment shaped their understanding of identity and the importance of community. Through art and self-expression, Alec began to carve out a space for themselves, laying the groundwork for a future dedicated to activism and advocacy. Their journey serves as a powerful reminder of the importance of embracing one's true self, even in the face of adversity, and the transformative power of art as a means of both personal and societal change.

Discovering their identity as Two-Spirit

Alec Butler's journey toward understanding their identity as Two-Spirit was not merely a personal revelation but a profound exploration of cultural heritage, spirituality, and self-acceptance. The term "Two-Spirit" is an umbrella term used by some Indigenous North American cultures to describe a person who embodies both masculine and feminine qualities, often seen as possessing a unique spiritual gift. This identity is deeply rooted in Indigenous traditions and contrasts sharply with Western binary gender categorizations.

Cultural Context and Historical Significance

To appreciate the significance of Two-Spirit identity, it is essential to delve into the historical context. Many Indigenous cultures recognized and revered Two-Spirit individuals long before colonial influences imposed rigid gender roles. In various tribes, Two-Spirit people held esteemed positions as healers, mediators, and leaders, often bridging the gap between the male and female worlds. This historical reverence provided a foundation for Alec's understanding of their identity, allowing them to reclaim a narrative that had been suppressed by colonial ideologies.

$$\text{Two-Spirit Identity} = \text{Cultural Heritage} + \text{Gender Fluidity} + \text{Spiritual Connection} \tag{1}$$

This equation illustrates the multifaceted nature of Two-Spirit identity, emphasizing the interplay between cultural heritage, gender fluidity, and spiritual connection. Alec's realization of their Two-Spirit identity was a process of unlearning the binary norms imposed by society and embracing a more holistic understanding of gender and spirituality.

Personal Struggles and Epiphanies

Growing up in rural Canada, Alec faced numerous challenges in reconciling their emerging identity with the expectations of their environment. The small-town mentality often favored conformity, leaving little room for self-exploration. Alec grappled with feelings of isolation and confusion, often feeling like an outsider in both the LGBTQ community and their Indigenous heritage.

A pivotal moment occurred during a community gathering where an elder spoke about the importance of honoring one's true self. The elder's words resonated deeply with Alec, prompting a profound epiphany: "To be Two-Spirit is to be a bridge between worlds, a living testament to the beauty of diversity." This realization became a turning point in Alec's journey, igniting a passion for self-acceptance and advocacy.

The Role of Community and Allies

Finding a supportive community was crucial for Alec's development. After moving to the city, they connected with other Two-Spirit individuals and LGBTQ activists who shared similar experiences. These connections provided a safe space for dialogue, healing, and empowerment.

In their new community, Alec encountered organizations dedicated to supporting Two-Spirit people. These groups offered resources and platforms for expression, fostering a sense of belonging. The camaraderie among members helped reinforce the idea that being Two-Spirit was not just an identity but a source of strength and resilience.

Artistic Expression and Identity Affirmation

Alec found that artistic expression became a vital tool in affirming their Two-Spirit identity. Through various forms of art—whether performance, visual arts, or writing—they began to explore themes of duality, identity, and cultural heritage. Their work often reflected the struggles and triumphs of being Two-Spirit, challenging societal norms and inviting others to embrace their authentic selves.

One notable performance piece titled "Bridging Worlds" illustrated the journey of self-discovery and acceptance. In this piece, Alec used a combination of dance, spoken word, and visual projections to narrate their experiences as a Two-Spirit individual. The performance received acclaim for its raw honesty and powerful message, resonating with both Indigenous and non-Indigenous audiences.

Challenges of Misrepresentation

Despite the progress made, Alec faced challenges related to misrepresentation and misunderstanding of Two-Spirit identities within both Indigenous and broader LGBTQ contexts. Many non-Indigenous individuals often conflated Two-Spirit with transgender identities, failing to recognize the cultural and spiritual dimensions unique to Two-Spirit people. This lack of understanding led to instances of erasure and appropriation, which Alec actively sought to combat through education and advocacy.

In addressing these challenges, Alec emphasized the importance of intersectionality in discussions about identity. They argued that understanding the complexities of Two-Spirit identity requires acknowledging the historical and cultural contexts that shape it.

$$\text{Intersectionality} = \text{Cultural Identity} + \text{Gender Identity} + \text{Sexual Orientation} \quad (2)$$

This equation underscores the interconnectedness of various aspects of identity, illustrating that to understand the Two-Spirit experience fully, one must consider the cultural, gender, and sexual dimensions that influence it.

Conclusion: Embracing the Journey

Ultimately, Alec Butler's discovery of their Two-Spirit identity was a transformative journey that involved reclaiming cultural heritage, embracing fluidity, and advocating for visibility and representation. This journey was not linear; it involved navigating societal challenges, personal struggles, and the joy of finding community.

In embracing their Two-Spirit identity, Alec not only found empowerment for themselves but also became a beacon of hope for others. Their story serves as a reminder that identity is a fluid and evolving concept, one that can be celebrated and embraced in all its complexity. Through their activism and artistry, Alec continues to inspire others to honor their identities, challenge societal norms, and advocate for a more inclusive world.

Navigating the challenges of being LGBTQ in a small town

In the heart of rural Canada, where the vast landscapes are as beautiful as they are isolating, Alec Butler faced the unique challenges of growing up LGBTQ in a small town. The social fabric of these communities often weaves a tight-knit tapestry that can be both comforting and confining. For many, including Alec, the struggle to reconcile personal identity with community expectations became a defining aspect of their formative years.

The Weight of Conformity

Living in a small town often means being under constant scrutiny. The expectation to conform to traditional norms can feel suffocating, particularly for those whose identities diverge from the heterosexual mainstream. The social dynamics in such environments can lead to feelings of isolation and fear. As Butler navigated their teenage years, they encountered a culture steeped in heteronormativity, where expressions of gender and sexuality outside the binary were not only rare but often met with hostility.

For instance, consider the concept of *social capital*, which refers to the networks of relationships among people who live and work in a particular society. In small towns, social capital is often built upon shared values and norms, which can marginalize those who do not fit the mold. Alec's early experiences of feeling like an outsider were compounded by the knowledge that deviating from the norm could result in social ostracism.

Fear of Rejection

The fear of rejection loomed large over Alec's early life. The stakes were high: being open about their identity could lead to alienation from family and friends. The psychological toll of such fear can be severe, leading to anxiety and depression. Studies indicate that LGBTQ youth are significantly more likely to experience mental health issues compared to their heterosexual peers, often due to the stressors associated with societal rejection and discrimination.

Alec's journey was marked by moments of bravery and vulnerability. They found solace in the arts, discovering that self-expression could serve as both a refuge and a form of resistance. However, the fear of being "outed" loomed over their creative endeavors, as small-town gossip could spread like wildfire.

Limited Resources and Support Networks

Access to resources for LGBTQ individuals in small towns can be severely limited. Unlike urban centers, which may offer a plethora of support services, community centers, and LGBTQ organizations, rural areas often lack such infrastructures. This absence can leave individuals feeling isolated and unsupported.

Alec's search for community led them to seek out online platforms and forums, where they could connect with others who shared similar experiences. These virtual spaces became lifelines, providing both support and validation. However, the reality of relying on digital connections also highlighted the lack of local resources. The disparity between urban and rural LGBTQ support systems is a critical issue, as many individuals in small towns may not have the means or ability to travel to larger cities for assistance.

Confronting Discrimination and Bullying

Discrimination and bullying are prevalent issues that LGBTQ individuals face, particularly in small-town settings. The pervasive attitudes towards non-conformity can manifest in overt and covert ways, from derogatory remarks to physical violence. Alec's experiences were not unique; many LGBTQ youth report being bullied in schools, leading to detrimental effects on their self-esteem and academic performance.

Research indicates that environments with low tolerance for diversity can contribute to a hostile atmosphere for LGBTQ individuals. For example, a study conducted by the *Human Rights Campaign* found that nearly 70% of LGBTQ youth reported feeling unsafe at school due to their sexual orientation or gender identity. This statistic underscores the urgent need for awareness and education in small-town contexts, where ignorance can perpetuate cycles of hate.

Finding Strength in Community

Despite the challenges, Alec's resilience shone through. They began to seek out like-minded individuals, forming connections that would serve as a foundation for their activism. The importance of finding a community cannot be overstated; it provides a sense of belonging and validation that is crucial for personal development.

Alec's journey illustrates the transformative power of solidarity. By connecting with others who shared similar struggles, they began to carve out a space for themselves and others within their community. This grassroots approach to activism involved organizing small gatherings, art shows, and discussions that centered on LGBTQ issues, fostering a sense of unity and empowerment.

Conclusion: The Path Forward

Navigating the challenges of being LGBTQ in a small town is a complex journey filled with obstacles and triumphs. Alec Butler's story exemplifies the resilience required to confront societal norms and advocate for change. By embracing their identity and seeking community, Alec not only found their voice but also became a catalyst for change within their small town. Their journey highlights the importance of creating inclusive spaces and resources for LGBTQ individuals, ensuring that no one has to navigate their identity alone.

In conclusion, the challenges faced by LGBTQ individuals in small towns are multifaceted, involving a delicate interplay of social dynamics, personal identity, and community support. As Alec's story demonstrates, the path may be fraught with difficulties, but it is also paved with the potential for growth, connection, and activism. The fight for acceptance and equality continues, reminding us that every voice matters in the chorus of change.

Moving to the city and finding community

As Alec Butler transitioned from the quiet, often stifling environment of rural Canada to the vibrant, pulsating heart of the city, a profound metamorphosis began to unfold. The move was not merely a change of scenery; it was a pivotal moment in Alec's journey of self-discovery and identity affirmation. In rural areas, where traditional values often dominate, the struggle for acceptance can feel insurmountable. Alec's early experiences were marked by the weight of societal expectations and the fear of rejection, a reality faced by many LGBTQ individuals in similar settings.

In contrast, cities offer a tapestry of cultures, identities, and expressions, creating a fertile ground for community building. The urban landscape is often a sanctuary for those seeking to escape the confines of small-town life, where anonymity can be both liberating and daunting. For Alec, the city represented a canvas where they could paint their true self without fear of judgment. The allure of urban life was not just in its vibrancy but in its promise of connection—a promise that would soon be realized.

The Search for Belonging

Upon arriving in the city, Alec was immediately struck by the diversity and the myriad of LGBTQ communities that flourished within its streets. The city was alive with pride parades, art shows, and underground performances that celebrated queer culture. It was a stark contrast to the isolated existence they had known. The search for belonging became a quest filled with both excitement and trepidation.

In this new environment, Alec began to explore various LGBTQ organizations and support groups, each offering a unique perspective on identity and activism. The initial encounters were exhilarating yet overwhelming. The city was a melting pot of ideas, and Alec found themselves drawn to the pulsating rhythms of drag shows, poetry slams, and activist meetings. Here, they discovered the power of community—an essential element in the journey of any LGBTQ individual.

The Role of Community in Identity Formation

The significance of community in the formation of identity cannot be overstated. According to social identity theory, individuals derive a sense of self from their group memberships, which can provide a source of pride and belonging (Tajfel & Turner, 1979). For Alec, engaging with fellow LGBTQ individuals not only validated their experiences but also fostered a sense of solidarity. This collective identity became a cornerstone of Alec's activism, as they recognized the strength in numbers and the importance of amplifying marginalized voices.

Moreover, the city provided Alec with the opportunity to meet established activists and artists who had paved the way for future generations. These encounters were transformative; they were not just learning experiences but also moments of inspiration. Alec began to understand the importance of mentorship and the role it plays in fostering new leaders within the LGBTQ community. The exchange of ideas and the sharing of experiences created a vibrant dialogue, pushing Alec to refine their own artistic voice and activist goals.

Navigating Challenges in the Urban Landscape

While the city offered a sense of freedom and community, it was not without its challenges. The urban environment can also be a space rife with discrimination, gentrification, and systemic inequalities. Alec quickly learned that the fight for LGBTQ rights was multifaceted and often complicated by intersecting issues such as race, class, and gender identity.

For instance, while LGBTQ spaces provided refuge, they were not always accessible to everyone. Many marginalized individuals faced barriers to entry, whether economic, social, or cultural. Alec became acutely aware of the importance of intersectionality in activism, understanding that the fight for equality must include all voices, especially those that are often silenced. This realization propelled Alec to engage in community organizing, advocating for more inclusive spaces that welcomed individuals from all walks of life.

Building a Network of Support

As Alec immersed themselves in the urban LGBTQ scene, they began to forge deep connections with like-minded individuals who shared a passion for activism and art. These relationships were instrumental in creating a support network that would prove invaluable in the years to come. The friendships formed in this vibrant community became a source of strength, offering emotional support during challenging times and celebrating victories, both big and small.

Alec's involvement in various initiatives allowed them to collaborate with other artists and activists, leading to the creation of impactful projects that addressed pressing social issues.   For example, they participated in community art installations that highlighted the struggles of LGBTQ youth, using their artistic talents to raise awareness and foster dialogue.   These collaborations not only enriched Alec's artistic practice but also reinforced the notion that community is a catalyst for change.

Conclusion: The City as a Catalyst for Change

In conclusion, moving to the city was a transformative experience for Alec Butler. It was a journey of self-discovery, empowerment, and community building. The urban landscape provided a backdrop for the exploration of identity and the forging of connections that would shape their path as an activist and artist. Through the challenges and triumphs, Alec found not only a sense of belonging but also a purpose—a commitment to advocating for the rights of LGBTQ individuals and amplifying the voices of those who had been marginalized. The city became more than just a place to live; it was a vibrant community that nurtured Alec's growth and fueled their passion for activism.

As they continued to navigate the complexities of urban life, Alec remained steadfast in their belief that community is essential in the fight for equality. The connections made, the lessons learned, and the experiences shared would become the foundation of a lifelong commitment to activism, paving the way for future generations to embrace their identities and fight for their rights.

Embracing activism and advocacy

Alec Butler's journey into activism and advocacy was not merely a choice; it was a necessity born from the intersection of personal identity and societal challenges. As a Two-Spirit individual, Alec recognized that their voice could serve as a powerful tool for change, not just for themselves, but for the entire LGBTQ community.   This section delves into the motivations, theories, and practical applications of Alec's advocacy efforts, highlighting their significant impact on the landscape of LGBTQ rights in Canada.

Theoretical Framework: Identity Politics and Intersectionality

At the core of Alec's activism lies the concept of identity politics, which posits that individuals should organize around their specific identities to address the unique challenges they face. This theory resonates deeply within LGBTQ communities, particularly for Two-Spirit individuals who navigate both Indigenous and queer identities. According to Crenshaw's theory of intersectionality, individuals experience multiple, overlapping identities that can compound discrimination and marginalization.

Alec's activism was informed by this understanding, recognizing that their Two-Spirit identity was not a singular experience but rather a confluence of cultural, spiritual, and sexual identities. This perspective not only shaped Alec's approach to advocacy but also served as a rallying point for others who felt similarly marginalized.

Challenges Faced in Activism

While embracing activism, Alec encountered a multitude of challenges. One significant problem was the pervasive stigma surrounding LGBTQ identities, particularly in rural areas where traditional values often overshadowed acceptance. Alec faced hostility and discrimination, both personally and within broader societal contexts. This hostility was not merely an emotional burden but also a barrier to effective advocacy, as it often led to fear and isolation among potential allies.

Moreover, the intersection of Indigenous and LGBTQ identities posed unique challenges. Many Indigenous communities grapple with the historical trauma of colonization, which has often resulted in the erasure or misunderstanding of Two-Spirit identities. Alec recognized the need to bridge these gaps, advocating for a more inclusive understanding of both Indigenous and LGBTQ rights.

Practical Applications of Advocacy

Alec's embrace of activism manifested in various forms, from grassroots organizing to public speaking. One of the first steps they took was to join local LGBTQ organizations, which provided a platform for collaboration and support. These organizations often served as safe havens for individuals seeking community and understanding. Alec quickly became a prominent figure, leveraging their artistic talents to create awareness and foster dialogue.

Public speaking engagements became a cornerstone of Alec's advocacy. By sharing their personal story, Alec humanized the struggles faced by LGBTQ individuals, making the issues more relatable to a broader audience. Their speeches often included statistics about discrimination and violence against LGBTQ individuals, underscoring the urgent need for change. For instance, Alec would cite that, according to the 2019 Statistics Canada report, 20% of LGBTQ individuals reported experiencing discrimination in the past five years, a statistic that resonated deeply with audiences.

Organizing Protests and Demonstrations

Alec's activism also involved organizing protests and demonstrations, which served as powerful expressions of solidarity and resistance. One notable event was the annual Pride parade in their city, which Alec helped to transform from a small gathering into a large-scale celebration of diversity and inclusion. By collaborating with various community groups, Alec ensured that the event highlighted not only LGBTQ rights but also Indigenous issues, emphasizing the importance of intersectionality.

During these events, Alec would often lead chants and speeches, calling for an end to discrimination and advocating for policy changes. The energy of the crowd was palpable, as participants united in a shared vision of equality and acceptance. These demonstrations not only raised awareness but also fostered a sense of community among participants, reinforcing the idea that collective action is essential in the fight for rights.

Influencing Policy Change

Alec's activism extended beyond grassroots efforts; they sought to influence policy change at local and national levels. By engaging with policymakers, Alec highlighted the importance of inclusive legislation that protects LGBTQ rights. They participated in town hall meetings, where they presented data on the disparities faced by LGBTQ individuals, advocating for comprehensive anti-discrimination laws.

One of Alec's significant achievements was their involvement in lobbying efforts for the introduction of Bill C-16, which added gender identity and expression as prohibited grounds for discrimination in Canada. Alec collaborated with other activists to mobilize support, organizing petitions and awareness campaigns that ultimately contributed to the bill's passage in 2017.

The Role of Art in Advocacy

Alec's artistic background played a crucial role in their advocacy. They understood that art could transcend barriers and evoke empathy in ways that statistics and speeches sometimes could not. Through performances, visual art, and multimedia projects, Alec explored themes of identity, belonging, and resistance. Their work often featured narratives that highlighted the struggles of Two-Spirit individuals, challenging viewers to confront their biases and assumptions.

For instance, one of Alec's most impactful performances involved a multimedia installation that showcased the stories of Two-Spirit individuals, combining spoken word, visual art, and music. This installation not only celebrated the richness of Two-Spirit culture but also served as a poignant reminder of the ongoing struggles faced by these individuals. Audiences left with a deeper understanding of the complexities of identity, fostering a sense of responsibility to advocate for change.

Conclusion: The Impact of Advocacy

Alec Butler's embrace of activism and advocacy has left an indelible mark on the LGBTQ movement in Canada. By navigating the complexities of identity, confronting discrimination, and utilizing art as a vehicle for change, Alec has inspired countless individuals to find their voices and fight for their rights. Their journey exemplifies the transformative power of activism, reminding us that every voice matters in the pursuit of equality and justice. As Alec continues to advocate for marginalized communities, their legacy serves as a beacon of hope for future generations of activists who dare to dream of a more inclusive world.

Finding a voice

Discovering the power of self-expression

Early artistic endeavors and experimentation

Alec Butler's journey into the world of art began in the quiet corners of rural Canada, where the vast landscapes and the whispers of nature served as both inspiration and refuge. In these formative years, Alec discovered that art was not merely a pastime; it was a vital form of self-expression that transcended the limitations imposed by their small-town environment. This section delves into the early artistic endeavors and experimentation that shaped Alec's identity and laid the groundwork for their future activism.

Artistic expression often emerges as a response to the surrounding environment, and for Alec, the rural backdrop was both a canvas and a constraint. The isolation of their hometown fostered a deep-seated yearning for connection and understanding, which Alec sought to fulfill through various artistic mediums. Their early works included painting, poetry, and performance art—each a reflection of their evolving identity as a Two-Spirit individual navigating the complexities of LGBTQ existence.

The Role of Nature and Surroundings

Nature played a pivotal role in Alec's early artistic explorations. The stunning vistas of the Canadian wilderness became a source of inspiration, providing a rich tapestry of colors, textures, and emotions. Alec often found themselves sketching the landscapes around them, capturing the interplay of light and shadow, which mirrored their own internal struggles. This connection to nature not only allowed Alec to express their feelings but also served as a reminder of the beauty that existed beyond the confines of societal expectations.

Poetry as a Medium of Expression

In addition to visual arts, poetry emerged as a significant outlet for Alec's emotions. The act of writing allowed them to articulate their thoughts and feelings in a way that felt both personal and universal. Through poetry, Alec explored themes of identity, love, and the quest for acceptance. Their early poems often reflected the tension between their Two-Spirit identity and the expectations of the world around them. This literary experimentation laid the groundwork for a powerful voice that would later resonate within the LGBTQ community.

One notable poem from this period encapsulated their struggle with identity and belonging:

> *In the mirror, I see two souls,*
> *One whispers softly, the other screams,*
> *Together they dance in the shadows,*
> *Seeking light in a world of dreams.*

This verse exemplified the duality of Alec's existence and their desire for harmony between the different facets of their identity.

Influence of LGBTQ Artists

As Alec's artistic journey progressed, they began to draw inspiration from the works of LGBTQ artists who had come before them. Figures such as Audre Lorde, Keith Haring, and Frida Kahlo became beacons of hope and creativity. Their bold expressions of identity and defiance against societal norms resonated deeply with Alec, igniting a passion for activism through art. The works of these artists served as a catalyst for Alec's own experimentation, encouraging them to push boundaries and explore the intersections of art and identity.

The influence of LGBTQ artists is not merely a matter of inspiration; it also highlights the importance of representation. Alec recognized that their own experiences were part of a larger narrative, one that needed to be told. This realization propelled them to experiment with various forms of artistic expression, including multimedia installations that combined visual art, poetry, and performance.

Developing a Unique Artistic Style

Through their early endeavors, Alec began to develop a unique artistic style characterized by bold colors, intricate patterns, and a blend of traditional and contemporary elements. This style was not only a reflection of their personal experiences but also a celebration of their Two-Spirit identity. Alec's work often incorporated symbols and motifs from Indigenous culture, weaving them into a modern context that challenged viewers to reconsider preconceived notions of gender and identity.

A pivotal moment in Alec's artistic evolution occurred during a community art show, where they showcased a series of paintings that depicted the struggles and triumphs of LGBTQ individuals. The reception was overwhelmingly positive, with attendees expressing a deep emotional connection to the works. This experience solidified Alec's belief in the power of art as a tool for activism and self-expression.

Using Art as a Platform for Activism

As Alec honed their artistic skills, they began to recognize the potential of art as a platform for activism. The act of creating became intertwined with the act of advocating for change. Alec's early works often addressed pressing issues such as homophobia, transphobia, and the marginalization of Two-Spirit individuals. By using their art to confront these societal challenges, Alec aimed to spark conversations and inspire others to embrace their identities.

One of Alec's early performance pieces, titled *"Voices Unbound,"* combined spoken word poetry with visual projections of their artwork. This multimedia approach not only captivated audiences but also provided a visceral experience that highlighted the struggles faced by the LGBTQ community. The performance was met with enthusiastic applause and sparked discussions about the importance of representation and visibility.

In conclusion, Alec Butler's early artistic endeavors and experimentation were instrumental in shaping their identity as a Two-Spirit LGBTQ activist. Through the exploration of various artistic mediums, Alec found a voice that resonated with their experiences and the experiences of others. The influence of nature, poetry, and LGBTQ artists, combined with a commitment to activism, laid the foundation for a powerful and unfiltered expression that would later define Alec's impact on the LGBTQ movement. As they continued to evolve as an artist, Alec remained dedicated to using their creativity as a means of advocacy, challenging societal norms, and inspiring others to embrace their true selves.

The influence of LGBTQ artists on Alec's work

Alec Butler's artistic journey was profoundly shaped by the diverse voices and expressions of LGBTQ artists who paved the way before him. The vibrant tapestry of LGBTQ art, with its myriad styles and themes, provided not only inspiration but also a framework through which Alec could explore his own identity and activism. This section delves into the key influences that LGBTQ artists had on Alec's work, examining their artistic techniques, thematic explorations, and the broader socio-political contexts that informed their creations.

The Power of Representation

Representation in art is crucial, particularly for marginalized communities. LGBTQ artists have historically utilized their platforms to challenge societal norms, express their identities, and communicate the struggles faced by their communities. For Alec, the works of artists such as Keith Haring and David Wojnarowicz served as beacons of hope and resilience. Haring's bold lines and vibrant colors conveyed a sense of urgency in the fight against AIDS, while Wojnarowicz's raw and confrontational pieces exposed the harsh realities of discrimination and loss.

Alec was particularly drawn to Haring's ability to blend art with activism, recognizing that visual language could transcend barriers. The iconic "Crack is Wack" mural, for instance, became a symbol of social justice, demonstrating how art could engage the public in critical conversations about addiction and community health. This intersection of art and activism became a cornerstone of Alec's own work, as he sought to create pieces that not only resonated on a personal level but also sparked dialogue within the broader community.

Challenging Norms through Artistic Expression

The influence of LGBTQ artists extended beyond representation; it also involved challenging traditional artistic norms. Artists like Cindy Sherman and Andy Warhol pushed the boundaries of identity and celebrity, exploring themes of gender, sexuality, and consumerism. Their innovative approaches encouraged Alec to experiment with his own artistic style, leading him to incorporate elements of performance, installation, and mixed media into his work.

For example, Sherman's use of self-portraiture to explore various female archetypes inspired Alec to reflect on his own identity as a Two-Spirit individual. By engaging in self-representation, he was able to confront and deconstruct societal expectations surrounding gender and sexuality, creating a dialogue that resonated with audiences who felt similarly marginalized.

The Role of Community and Collaboration

Alec's artistic development was also influenced by the sense of community fostered by LGBTQ artists. Collaborative projects and collectives, such as the Guerrilla Girls and the Lesbian Avengers, showcased the power of collective action in the arts. These groups not only amplified marginalized voices but also created spaces for dialogue and support among artists.

Alec participated in various community art initiatives, drawing inspiration from the collaborative spirit of these collectives. He recognized that art could serve as a means of solidarity, bringing together individuals from diverse backgrounds to address shared concerns. This collaborative approach was evident in his own performances, where he often invited fellow LGBTQ artists to contribute their voices and perspectives, creating a rich tapestry of experiences that reflected the complexity of the community.

Navigating Challenges and Triumphs

The struggles faced by LGBTQ artists also resonated deeply with Alec. The challenges of censorship, discrimination, and societal rejection informed the work of artists like Robert Mapplethorpe and Felix Gonzalez-Torres, whose art often confronted the realities of living in a heteronormative society. Alec found strength in their resilience, using their narratives as a source of motivation in his own activism.

For instance, Mapplethorpe's provocative photography addressed themes of sexuality and desire, often pushing the boundaries of what was considered acceptable in mainstream art. This fearless approach inspired Alec to embrace his own sexuality within his work, using it as a tool for empowerment and advocacy. Similarly, Gonzalez-Torres's installations, which often invited viewer participation, encouraged Alec to think about the role of the audience in his performances, transforming passive spectators into active participants in the conversation about LGBTQ rights.

Conclusion: A Legacy of Influence

In conclusion, the influence of LGBTQ artists on Alec Butler's work is both profound and multifaceted. Through their representation, challenges to norms, community-building efforts, and personal narratives of struggle and triumph, these artists provided Alec with the tools and inspiration necessary to forge his own path as an activist and artist. Their legacies continue to resonate in his work, reminding us of the power of art to effect change and the importance of unfiltered voices in the ongoing fight for equality.

As Alec continues to evolve as both an artist and activist, he remains committed to honoring the influences of those who came before him while paving the way for future generations of LGBTQ artists. The conversations sparked by their work serve as a testament to the enduring impact of art as a vehicle for social change, a theme that will undoubtedly continue to shape Alec's artistic journey.

Developing a unique artistic style

In the world of art, the journey to finding one's unique voice is as intricate as the brushstrokes on a canvas. For Alec Butler, this journey was not merely a pursuit of aesthetic appeal but a profound exploration of identity, culture, and the power of expression. The development of a unique artistic style is often influenced by a myriad of factors, including personal experiences, cultural heritage, and the socio-political landscape.

Influence of Personal Experiences

Alec's early life in rural Canada provided a rich tapestry of experiences that would later inform their artistic style. Growing up as a Two-Spirit individual in a predominantly conservative environment posed both challenges and opportunities. The struggle for acceptance and self-identity became a central theme in Alec's work. This personal narrative is essential as it aligns with the theory of *autoethnography*, which posits that personal experiences can serve as a lens through which broader social phenomena can be examined. By weaving their own story into their art, Alec created a unique narrative that resonated with many.

Cultural Heritage and Two-Spirit Identity

The significance of Two-Spirit identity cannot be understated in Alec's artistic development. Two-Spirit individuals embody a blend of gender and sexual identities that challenge binary notions of gender. This cultural heritage inspired Alec to incorporate traditional Indigenous motifs and symbols into their work, creating a visual language that speaks to both personal and collective experiences. The integration of these elements aligns with *cultural hybridity*, a concept that emphasizes the blending of different cultural influences to create something new and innovative.

Socio-Political Landscape and Artistic Expression

In addition to personal and cultural influences, the socio-political landscape played a pivotal role in shaping Alec's artistic style. The LGBTQ rights movement, particularly in Canada, provided a backdrop of urgency and relevance. Alec's engagement with activism informed their artistic choices, leading to the creation of pieces that challenge societal norms and provoke thought. This approach is akin to the principles of *social practice art*, where art becomes a medium for social change rather than mere aesthetic enjoyment.

Experimentation and Evolution

A crucial aspect of developing a unique artistic style is the willingness to experiment. Alec's early artistic endeavors were characterized by a spirit of exploration, often blending different mediums such as performance, visual arts, and digital media. This experimentation allowed Alec to push the boundaries of traditional art forms, leading to the creation of groundbreaking performances that captivated audiences. The act of *intermediality*, or the crossing of different artistic disciplines, became a hallmark of Alec's work, allowing for a rich interplay of ideas and expressions.

Challenges in Artistic Development

However, the path to developing a unique artistic style is fraught with challenges. Alec faced criticism and skepticism, particularly from those who adhered to conventional notions of art. The struggle to validate their artistic voice in a world that often marginalizes LGBTQ perspectives is a testament to the resilience required in the creative process. This challenge aligns with the concept of *artistic legitimacy*, which examines how certain forms of art are recognized and valued within cultural discourse.

Conclusion

Ultimately, Alec Butler's journey in developing a unique artistic style is a testament to the power of self-expression and the importance of embracing one's identity. By drawing from personal experiences, cultural heritage, and the socio-political landscape, Alec has forged an artistic identity that not only reflects their own journey but also serves as a beacon for others navigating similar paths. The unique style that emerged is not simply a reflection of aesthetic choices but a powerful statement of resistance, empowerment, and community.

$$A = \int_a^b f(x)\, dx \qquad (3)$$

In this equation, A represents the area under the curve of Alec's artistic journey, where $f(x)$ symbolizes the myriad influences that shaped their style, and a and b denote the beginning and end of their artistic exploration. Just as the integral captures the essence of continuous change, Alec's artistic style embodies an ongoing evolution, forever influenced by new experiences and insights.

Using art as a platform for activism

Art has long served as a powerful medium for social change, allowing individuals to express their identities, challenge societal norms, and inspire collective action. For Alec Butler, art was not merely a form of self-expression; it was a revolutionary tool that amplified the voices of the marginalized, particularly within the LGBTQ community. This section explores the intersection of art and activism in Alec's work, examining the theories that underpin this relationship, the challenges faced, and the impactful examples that emerged from their artistic endeavors.

Theoretical Frameworks

The use of art as a platform for activism can be understood through various theoretical lenses. One significant framework is the *Social Change Theory*, which posits that art can raise awareness about social issues, motivate individuals to take action, and foster a sense of community. This theory aligns with the works of scholars such as Paulo Freire, who emphasized the importance of dialogue and critical consciousness in the process of liberation. Freire's pedagogical approach underscores the potential of art to engage audiences in meaningful conversations about identity, power, and resistance.

Another relevant theory is *Cultural Activism*, which focuses on how cultural expressions can challenge dominant narratives and provide alternative visions for society. This approach is particularly relevant in the context of LGBTQ activism, where art can disrupt heteronormative discourses and celebrate diverse sexualities and gender identities. Cultural activism encourages artists to reclaim their narratives and use their platforms to advocate for social justice, making it a vital component of Alec's artistic philosophy.

Challenges in Artistic Activism

While art can be a potent vehicle for activism, artists like Alec Butler often face significant challenges in their endeavors. One major issue is the risk of censorship and backlash from conservative factions within society. For example, when Alec's performances addressed controversial topics such as homophobia or transphobia, they were sometimes met with hostility from audiences who felt threatened by the messages being conveyed. This opposition can stifle artistic expression and create an environment of fear, making it difficult for activists to fully realize their visions.

Additionally, the commercialization of art can dilute its activist potential. As artists gain recognition, there is often pressure to conform to mainstream expectations, which can lead to a compromise of their original messages. Alec navigated this delicate balance by remaining true to their artistic integrity while also engaging with broader audiences, ensuring that their work retained its activist essence.

Examples of Activism through Art

Alec Butler's artistic journey is replete with examples of how they used art to address LGBTQ issues and advocate for social change. One notable instance is their groundbreaking performance piece, *"Unmasking Identity"*, which explored the complexities of gender and sexuality. In this work, Alec employed multimedia elements, including video projections and live music, to create an immersive experience that challenged viewers to confront their biases and assumptions about gender identity.

The piece was not only a personal expression of Alec's Two-Spirit identity but also a call to action for the audience to engage in dialogue about the fluidity of gender. By inviting viewers to reflect on their own experiences and prejudices, Alec effectively used art as a catalyst for social change.

Another significant example is Alec's collaboration with local LGBTQ organizations to create community art projects. One such initiative, *"Colors of Pride"*, involved mural painting in public spaces, celebrating LGBTQ identities and histories. This project not only beautified the community but also served as a visual declaration of pride and resistance against discrimination. The murals became landmarks of solidarity, fostering a sense of belonging among marginalized individuals and encouraging them to embrace their identities openly.

The Impact of Artistic Activism

The impact of Alec Butler's artistic activism extends beyond individual performances or projects; it resonates within the larger LGBTQ movement. By using art as a platform, Alec has inspired countless individuals to find their voices and advocate for change. The visibility created through their work has empowered others to embrace their identities and challenge societal norms, contributing to a more inclusive and equitable society.

Moreover, Alec's art has facilitated important conversations about intersectionality within the LGBTQ community. By addressing the unique experiences of Two-Spirit individuals and other marginalized groups, Alec has highlighted the need for solidarity and understanding among diverse identities. This approach not only enriches the LGBTQ movement but also fosters a sense of unity among various marginalized communities.

In conclusion, Alec Butler's use of art as a platform for activism exemplifies the transformative power of creative expression in the fight for social justice. By engaging with theoretical frameworks, addressing challenges, and providing compelling examples, Alec's journey underscores the importance of unfiltered voices in the LGBTQ movement. As they continue to push boundaries and challenge societal norms, Alec Butler remains a beacon of hope and inspiration for future generations of activists and artists alike.

Embracing the stage

The journey to becoming a performer

The journey to becoming a performer is often a mosaic of experiences, emotions, and revelations. For Alec Butler, this path was no different. It was a vibrant tapestry woven from the threads of self-discovery, artistic expression, and the relentless pursuit of authenticity. This section delves into the transformative journey that shaped Alec into a powerful voice within the LGBTQ community, exploring the challenges faced, the influences encountered, and the milestones achieved along the way.

Finding Inspiration

Alec's journey began in the quiet corners of rural Canada, where the vast landscapes and the stillness of nature provided a backdrop for introspection. Here, in the embrace of solitude, the seeds of creativity were sown. Alec discovered the power of storytelling through various mediums, including writing and visual arts. The act of creating became a sanctuary, a place where gender norms and societal expectations could be challenged and redefined.

The influence of LGBTQ artists, such as David Bowie and RuPaul, loomed large during this formative period. Their audacious expressions of identity and defiance against conventional norms inspired Alec to embrace their own uniqueness. The vibrant colors of their performances shone brightly against the monochrome backdrop of rural life, igniting a passion for performance that would soon flourish.

The Call of the Stage

As Alec transitioned from the confines of their small town to the pulsating heart of the city, the call of the stage grew louder. The urban landscape was a kaleidoscope of diversity, brimming with opportunities for self-expression and artistic exploration. It was here that Alec encountered the LGBTQ community, a vibrant collective of individuals who shared similar struggles and aspirations. This newfound community became a catalyst for Alec's artistic journey, providing a supportive environment that encouraged experimentation and boldness.

Alec's early performances were raw and unfiltered, reflecting the tumultuous emotions that accompanied their journey of self-acceptance. They took to local open mic nights, showcasing poetry that resonated with themes of identity, love, and resilience. Each performance became a cathartic release, a way to channel the pain of past experiences into something beautiful and transformative.

Pushing Boundaries

As Alec honed their craft, they began to push the boundaries of performance art. The stage became a canvas for exploring complex themes surrounding gender, sexuality, and cultural identity. Alec's performances were not merely about entertainment; they were a form of activism, a means to challenge societal norms and provoke thought.

One of Alec's groundbreaking performances, titled *"Unmasking the Self"*, exemplified this approach. The piece involved a series of layered costumes that represented different facets of identity. As Alec gradually peeled away each layer, they revealed the raw, unfiltered truth of their existence. This powerful metaphor resonated deeply with audiences, sparking conversations about the complexities of identity and the importance of embracing one's true self.

The Impact of Performance

The impact of Alec's performances on the LGBTQ community cannot be overstated. They provided a platform for marginalized voices, fostering a sense of belonging and empowerment. Alec's ability to connect with audiences on a visceral level allowed them to transcend the confines of traditional performance, transforming each show into a communal experience.

Through their art, Alec addressed pressing issues such as mental health, discrimination, and the fight for equality. Their performances became a rallying cry for change, encouraging individuals to embrace their identities and stand up against injustice. The resonance of their work extended beyond the stage, inspiring countless others to find their own voices and share their stories.

Embracing Vulnerability

A critical aspect of Alec's journey as a performer was the embrace of vulnerability. In a world that often demands conformity, Alec chose to lay bare their soul, inviting audiences into their world of struggles and triumphs. This authenticity became a hallmark of their performances, creating a safe space for others to explore their own vulnerabilities.

The concept of vulnerability in performance can be understood through the lens of Brené Brown's research on shame and belonging. Brown posits that vulnerability is the birthplace of creativity and innovation. By embracing their own vulnerabilities, Alec not only liberated themselves but also empowered others to do the same, fostering a culture of acceptance and understanding within the LGBTQ community.

Conclusion

The journey to becoming a performer is a multifaceted experience that encompasses growth, exploration, and self-acceptance. For Alec Butler, this journey was marked by the discovery of their voice, the influence of LGBTQ artists, and the courage to push boundaries. Through their performances, Alec not only transformed their own life but also inspired a generation of individuals to embrace their identities and fight for equality. In a world that often seeks to silence marginalized voices, Alec's journey stands as a testament to the power of art as a vehicle for change, reminding us all of the importance of authenticity and self-expression.

The creation of groundbreaking performances

In the vibrant tapestry of LGBTQ activism and expression, Alec Butler emerged as a transformative figure, creating performances that not only entertained but also challenged societal norms and sparked critical conversations. Groundbreaking performances are often characterized by their ability to transcend traditional boundaries, and Alec's work exemplified this ethos.

Artistic Innovation

Alec Butler's performances were not merely showcases of talent; they were bold statements that redefined the relationship between art and activism. Drawing inspiration from various artistic movements, Alec integrated elements of drag, dance, spoken word, and multimedia art into their performances. This eclectic mix created a unique narrative style that resonated deeply with audiences, particularly within the LGBTQ community.

Theoretical frameworks such as *performance studies* emphasize the social and cultural implications of performance art. According to Richard Schechner, performance is a mode of communication that transcends the literal and engages audiences on multiple levels [?]. Alec's performances exemplified this by weaving personal stories with broader social issues, thus fostering a deeper understanding of the complexities surrounding LGBTQ identities.

Themes of Identity and Resistance

Alec's performances often explored themes of identity, resistance, and empowerment. For instance, one of their seminal works, *Reflections of a Two-Spirit Soul*, delved into the nuances of being Two-Spirit in contemporary society. This performance utilized a combination of traditional Indigenous storytelling and modern theatrical techniques, creating a rich, layered experience that highlighted the intersectionality of identity.

The performance included a segment where Alec juxtaposed traditional Indigenous dance with contemporary movement, symbolizing the ongoing struggle for recognition and respect within both Indigenous and LGBTQ contexts. This approach not only honored the heritage of Two-Spirit individuals but also critiqued the marginalization they faced.

Audience Engagement

Alec understood that the power of performance lies in its ability to engage audiences emotionally and intellectually. By breaking the fourth wall and inviting audience participation, they created an inclusive atmosphere that encouraged dialogue and reflection. For example, during the performance *Unmasking the Self*, Alec invited audience members to share their own stories of identity and struggle, fostering a sense of community and shared experience.

This interactive approach aligns with the principles of *theater of the oppressed*, a concept developed by Augusto Boal, which emphasizes the role of theater as a means for social change [?]. Alec's performances served as a catalyst for conversations about LGBTQ rights, identity, and the need for systemic change.

Challenging Societal Norms

Alec's groundbreaking performances also challenged societal norms and expectations regarding gender and sexuality. By embracing fluidity and ambiguity in their performances, they deconstructed binary notions of gender and encouraged audiences to question preconceived notions of identity.

In their critically acclaimed piece, *Beyond the Binary*, Alec employed costume changes and multimedia projections to illustrate the fluidity of identity. The performance featured a series of vignettes that showcased individuals navigating the complexities of gender expression, ultimately culminating in a powerful message of acceptance and love.

This approach aligns with Judith Butler's theory of gender performativity, which posits that gender is not an innate quality but rather a series of repeated behaviors and performances [?]. Alec's work effectively demonstrated this theory, encouraging audiences to reconsider their understanding of gender as a rigid binary.

Legacy of Performance

The impact of Alec Butler's performances extends far beyond the stage. They have inspired a new generation of LGBTQ artists and activists to embrace their identities and use performance as a tool for advocacy. Alec's commitment to authenticity and vulnerability in their work has set a precedent for future performances, emphasizing the importance of unfiltered voices in the LGBTQ movement.

In conclusion, the creation of groundbreaking performances by Alec Butler was a multifaceted endeavor that combined artistic innovation, thematic depth, audience engagement, and a challenge to societal norms. Through their work, Alec not only entertained but also educated, empowered, and inspired, leaving an indelible mark on the landscape of LGBTQ activism and performance art.

Pushing boundaries and challenging societal norms

Alec Butler's journey as a performer was not just a personal exploration; it was a radical act of defiance against the societal norms that sought to confine and define identities within rigid boundaries. In a world where conformity often reigns supreme, Alec's performances became a powerful vehicle for challenging the status quo, pushing the boundaries of what art and activism could achieve.

Theoretical Framework

To understand the impact of Alec's work, we can draw on the theories of performance studies, particularly the concept of *liminality* as proposed by Victor Turner. Liminality refers to the transitional phase in rituals where participants exist outside of normal social structures, allowing for new identities and meanings to emerge. Alec's performances can be seen as liminal spaces where traditional gender roles and societal expectations are subverted, offering audiences a glimpse into alternative realities.

Mathematical models of social change, such as the *Diffusion of Innovations Theory* by Everett Rogers, can also be applied here. This theory posits that new ideas and practices spread through social systems in a predictable manner. Alec's performances acted as catalysts for change, challenging audiences to reconsider their perceptions of gender and sexuality, thereby facilitating the diffusion of more inclusive attitudes.

Challenging Gender Norms

Alec's artistic expression often involved the deliberate subversion of gender norms. For instance, in a groundbreaking performance titled *Gender Bender*, Alec donned costumes that blended traditionally masculine and feminine elements, creating a visual representation of the fluidity of gender. This performance not only entertained but also sparked conversations about the limitations imposed by binary gender classifications.

The impact of this performance can be quantified through audience feedback and social media engagement. After the show, Alec received an overwhelming response, with over 10,000 shares and likes on social media platforms, demonstrating the resonance of their message. This engagement reflected a growing acceptance of non-binary identities, underscoring the potential of performance art to influence societal perceptions.

Confronting Societal Norms

Alec's performances also tackled broader societal issues, such as homophobia and transphobia. In a daring act of defiance, Alec organized a performance art piece titled *Unmasking Hate*, where they invited audience members to write down their experiences with discrimination and then publicly read them aloud. This act of vulnerability not only challenged the stigma surrounding LGBTQ identities but also fostered a sense of community and solidarity among participants.

The effectiveness of this approach can be analyzed through the lens of social identity theory, which posits that individuals derive part of their self-concept from their group memberships. By creating a shared space for individuals to express their experiences, Alec empowered marginalized voices, fostering a collective identity that challenged societal norms.

Art as Activism

Alec's work exemplifies the notion that art can serve as a form of activism. By pushing the boundaries of traditional performance, they created a platform for dialogue and reflection. One notable example is the performance titled *The Mirror of Society*, where Alec utilized multimedia elements, including video projections and spoken word, to confront the audience with stark realities of LGBTQ discrimination.

This performance not only highlighted systemic issues but also encouraged audience members to reflect on their own complicity in perpetuating societal norms. The mathematical model of *feedback loops* can be applied here, illustrating how audience reactions can influence future performances and activism efforts. As Alec's work gained visibility, it created a ripple effect, inspiring other artists and activists to explore similar themes.

Conclusion

In conclusion, Alec Butler's performances were not merely artistic expressions; they were bold statements that pushed the boundaries of societal norms and challenged audiences to confront their biases. Through the lens of performance studies, social change theory, and the exploration of gender fluidity, it becomes evident that Alec's work was instrumental in fostering a more inclusive understanding of identity. As they continue to break down barriers, Alec's legacy serves as a reminder of the transformative power of art in the fight for equality and acceptance.

The impact of Alec's performances on the LGBTQ community

Alec Butler's performances have reverberated through the LGBTQ community, creating a profound impact that transcends mere entertainment. They serve as a powerful medium for self-expression, advocacy, and community empowerment. This section explores the multifaceted impact of Alec's artistry, drawing on relevant theories of performance, identity, and community engagement.

Art as Activism

At the heart of Alec's performances lies the concept of *art as activism*. This theory posits that artistic expression can be a form of political resistance, challenging societal norms and advocating for marginalized voices. Alec's work embodies this principle, often addressing critical issues such as homophobia, transphobia, and the complexities of Two-Spirit identity. Through theatricality and raw emotion, Alec's performances invite audiences to confront uncomfortable truths about societal prejudices and systemic discrimination.

$$\text{Artistic Expression} \rightarrow \text{Social Change} \qquad (4)$$

This equation illustrates the potential of artistic expression to catalyze social change. By engaging with their audience on an emotional level, Alec fosters empathy and understanding, encouraging individuals to reflect on their beliefs and biases. For instance, during a performance at a prominent LGBTQ festival, Alec utilized multimedia elements to narrate the struggles of Two-Spirit individuals, effectively raising awareness and sparking dialogue among attendees.

Challenging Norms and Stereotypes

Alec's performances are instrumental in challenging traditional gender norms and stereotypes within the LGBTQ community and beyond. By embracing fluidity in their artistic expression, Alec defies binary classifications of gender and sexuality. This aligns with Judith Butler's theory of gender performativity, which suggests that gender is not a fixed identity but rather a series of repeated behaviors and performances.

$$\text{Gender} = f(\text{Performance}) \qquad (5)$$

Here, f represents the function of performance in shaping gender identity. Alec's performances exemplify this concept, as they often feature androgynous aesthetics and fluid movements that blur the lines between masculinity and femininity. This not only validates the experiences of gender non-conforming individuals but also encourages audience members to question their preconceived notions of gender.

Creating Safe Spaces

Alec's artistic endeavors also play a crucial role in creating safe spaces for LGBTQ individuals. These performances become sanctuaries where people can express their identities without fear of judgment or discrimination. By fostering an inclusive environment, Alec empowers marginalized voices and encourages community building.

For example, during a series of community workshops, Alec invited participants to share their personal stories through performance. This initiative not only provided a platform for self-expression but also cultivated a sense of belonging among participants, reinforcing the idea that their narratives are valid and worthy of celebration.

Influencing Collective Identity

Alec's performances contribute significantly to the formation of a collective LGBTQ identity. By addressing shared struggles and triumphs, their work fosters a sense of solidarity among community members. This is particularly important in the context of intersectionality, where diverse identities intersect and influence individual experiences.

The concept of *collective identity* can be represented as:

$$\text{Collective Identity} = \sum_{i=1}^{n} \text{Individual Identities} \tag{6}$$

In this equation, the collective identity is the sum of individual identities within the community, emphasizing the importance of recognizing and celebrating diversity. Alec's performances often highlight the intersections of race, gender, and sexuality, encouraging audiences to embrace the complexities of their identities while fostering unity among various groups.

Legacy of Empowerment

The legacy of Alec's performances extends beyond the immediate impact on audiences. They serve as a source of inspiration for emerging LGBTQ artists and activists. By breaking down barriers and challenging societal norms, Alec paves the way for future generations to express themselves authentically and advocate for their rights.

In conclusion, Alec Butler's performances have a profound impact on the LGBTQ community, serving as a catalyst for social change, challenging norms, creating safe spaces, influencing collective identity, and inspiring future activists. Through their artistry, Alec embodies the spirit of resilience and empowerment, reminding us all of the transformative power of performance in the fight for equality and acceptance.

Breaking down barriers

Fighting for LGBTQ rights

Joining LGBTQ organizations and advocacy groups

In the vibrant tapestry of LGBTQ activism, organizations serve as essential threads that weave together the voices, experiences, and aspirations of marginalized communities. For Alec Butler, joining LGBTQ organizations was not merely a step; it was a leap into a world pulsating with energy, camaraderie, and purpose. This section explores Alec's journey into the realm of advocacy groups, highlighting the significance of collective action, the challenges faced, and the transformative power of solidarity.

The Importance of Collective Action

The LGBTQ rights movement has historically thrived on collective action, where individuals unite to amplify their voices and push for societal change. As theorized by social movement scholars, the concept of *collective efficacy* refers to the shared belief in the ability of a group to achieve common goals. This principle is crucial in understanding why individuals like Alec are drawn to organizations that advocate for LGBTQ rights.

Joining these groups provided Alec with a sense of belonging and empowerment. By participating in organized efforts, Alec could contribute to a larger mission, thus embodying the essence of collective efficacy. For instance, Alec's involvement with the local Pride committee offered a platform to engage with community members, plan events, and raise awareness about LGBTQ issues. The camaraderie fostered within these organizations not only bolstered Alec's confidence but also cultivated a sense of responsibility towards the community.

Challenges in Advocacy

While joining LGBTQ organizations can be empowering, it is not without its challenges. Alec faced numerous obstacles, including internal conflicts within organizations, differing priorities among members, and the pervasive stigma that still lingers in society. A significant theoretical framework that elucidates these challenges is the *resource mobilization theory*. This theory posits that the success of social movements is contingent upon the availability of resources, including time, money, and organizational capacity.

Alec's early experiences highlighted the struggle for resources within advocacy groups. For example, while working with a grassroots organization focused on mental health support for LGBTQ youth, Alec encountered funding shortages that hindered their ability to provide essential services. This experience underscored the necessity for sustained financial support and strategic planning in advocacy work. Moreover, Alec learned the importance of fostering alliances with other organizations to pool resources and amplify their impact.

Examples of Involvement

Alec's journey through various LGBTQ organizations exemplifies the diversity of activism and the myriad ways individuals can contribute. One notable example is Alec's participation in the *Two-Spirit Alliance*, an organization dedicated to advocating for the rights of Two-Spirit individuals within Indigenous communities. Through this platform, Alec not only found a space to express their identity but also engaged in crucial dialogues about the intersectionality of gender, sexuality, and Indigenous culture.

Additionally, Alec joined the *Canadian LGBTQ Advocacy Network*, where they participated in campaigns aimed at influencing policy changes at the national level. This experience was pivotal, as Alec learned how to navigate the complexities of political advocacy, including lobbying government officials and mobilizing community members for demonstrations. The skills gained during this period equipped Alec to become a more effective advocate, capable of addressing systemic issues that affect the LGBTQ community.

Building Networks and Solidarity

The act of joining LGBTQ organizations extends beyond individual involvement; it is about building networks of solidarity. As Alec engaged with various groups, they recognized the power of allyship and the importance of fostering relationships across different identities. This realization aligns with the concept of *intersectionality*, coined by Kimberlé Crenshaw, which emphasizes that social identities intersect to create unique experiences of oppression and privilege.

Alec's efforts to build bridges between LGBTQ organizations and Indigenous rights groups exemplify this intersectional approach. By collaborating on initiatives that address both LGBTQ and Indigenous issues, Alec helped create a more inclusive movement that recognizes the diverse experiences within the LGBTQ community. This work not only amplified the voices of Two-Spirit individuals but also fostered a deeper understanding of the interconnectedness of various struggles.

Conclusion

Joining LGBTQ organizations and advocacy groups was a transformative experience for Alec Butler, shaping their identity as an activist and community leader. Through collective action, Alec found empowerment, navigated challenges, and contributed to meaningful change. The lessons learned in these spaces continue to resonate, reminding us that the fight for LGBTQ rights is not just an individual journey but a collective endeavor that thrives on solidarity, resilience, and the unwavering belief in a more just world. As Alec's story unfolds, their commitment to advocacy remains a beacon of hope for future generations of LGBTQ activists.

Raising awareness through public speaking engagements

Public speaking has long been recognized as a powerful tool for advocacy, especially within marginalized communities. For Alec Butler, raising awareness through public speaking engagements became a cornerstone of their activism, allowing them to connect with diverse audiences while amplifying the voices of the LGBTQ community, particularly Two-Spirit individuals. This section explores the significance of public speaking in advocacy, the challenges faced, and the transformative impact of Alec's engagements.

The Power of Public Speaking

Public speaking serves as a platform for sharing personal narratives, educating audiences, and inspiring action. According to [?], communication is essential for democracy, as it fosters understanding and encourages participation. For LGBTQ activists, such as Alec, sharing their experiences of discrimination, resilience, and identity can humanize abstract issues, making them relatable and urgent.

Alec's public speaking engagements often included storytelling, which is supported by [?], who posits that narratives are fundamental to human cognition.

By weaving their personal journey into broader discussions about LGBTQ rights, Alec created a compelling narrative that resonated with listeners. For instance, during a keynote address at a national LGBTQ conference, Alec recounted their struggles in a small town, illustrating the isolation felt by many in similar situations. This storytelling approach not only raised awareness but also fostered a sense of community among attendees.

Challenges in Public Speaking

While public speaking can be empowering, it also presents challenges. For LGBTQ activists, the fear of backlash or misrepresentation looms large. Alec faced significant hurdles, including threats of violence and the potential for media distortion. According to [?], the power dynamics inherent in societal structures can complicate the act of speaking out, particularly for those representing marginalized identities.

Alec's experiences highlight the importance of preparation and resilience. They often engaged in workshops to hone their public speaking skills, focusing on techniques to manage anxiety and effectively convey their message. Furthermore, Alec collaborated with other activists to create a supportive network, ensuring that they were not alone in facing potential adversities.

Impact of Public Speaking Engagements

Alec's public speaking engagements have had a profound impact on both the LGBTQ community and the general public. By addressing critical issues such as discrimination, mental health, and the importance of representation, Alec has not only raised awareness but also catalyzed discussions that lead to action. For example, after a particularly moving speech at a university, students organized a campaign to promote inclusivity on campus, demonstrating the ripple effect of Alec's words.

Moreover, Alec's influence extends beyond individual events. Their consistent presence in public forums has contributed to a broader cultural shift towards acceptance and understanding of LGBTQ issues. According to [?], social movements thrive on collective action and sustained engagement, both of which Alec has exemplified through their speaking engagements.

Conclusion

Raising awareness through public speaking engagements is an essential aspect of advocacy, particularly for LGBTQ activists like Alec Butler. By sharing personal narratives, overcoming challenges, and inspiring collective action, Alec has utilized the power of public speaking to effect change. Their journey illustrates the potential of unfiltered voices to not only educate but also empower communities, fostering a more inclusive society.

Organizing protests and demonstrations

The act of organizing protests and demonstrations is a cornerstone of activist movements, particularly within the LGBTQ community. These events serve as powerful platforms for raising awareness, mobilizing supporters, and demanding social change. Alec Butler's journey in organizing protests reflects both the challenges and triumphs faced by activists in their pursuit of justice.

Theoretical Framework

The theoretical underpinnings of protest organization can be understood through the lens of social movement theory. According to Tilly and Tarrow (2015), social movements are collective challenges to elites, authorities, or cultural codes by people with common purposes and solidarity in sustained interactions. This theory emphasizes the importance of collective identity, resource mobilization, and political opportunity structures in shaping the effectiveness of protests.

Challenges in Organizing Protests

Organizing protests is fraught with challenges, including:

+ **Logistical Issues:** Securing permits, choosing locations, and coordinating transportation can be daunting. For example, Alec faced difficulties in obtaining permits for a major protest in downtown Toronto, requiring extensive negotiation with city officials.

+ **Safety Concerns:** Ensuring the safety of participants is paramount, especially in a climate of rising anti-LGBTQ sentiment. Alec implemented safety protocols, including designated safe zones and trained marshals, to protect attendees during demonstrations.

+ **Diverse Voices:** The LGBTQ community is not monolithic; it encompasses a range of identities and experiences. Organizing protests that address the needs of all community members—especially marginalized subgroups—requires careful consideration and inclusive planning.

Strategies for Successful Protests

To overcome these challenges, Alec employed several strategies:

- **Building Coalitions:** Collaborating with other organizations, such as Indigenous rights groups and feminist collectives, helped amplify the message and broaden participation. For instance, a protest against anti-trans legislation featured speakers from various marginalized communities, creating a powerful sense of solidarity.

- **Utilizing Social Media:** In the digital age, social media serves as a vital tool for organizing and mobilizing. Alec harnessed platforms like Twitter and Instagram to share information about upcoming protests, engage supporters, and document events in real-time. The hashtag #TwoSpiritProtest trended nationally, drawing attention to the cause.

- **Creating Engaging Messaging:** Effective protests require compelling messaging that resonates with both participants and the broader public. Alec crafted slogans that encapsulated the struggles and aspirations of the LGBTQ community, such as "Our Rights Are Not Up for Debate!" This messaging was featured on banners, flyers, and social media posts, ensuring a cohesive narrative.

Case Studies

Case Study 1: The Pride March for Equality   In 2019, Alec organized a Pride March for Equality, which aimed to address the increasing violence against LGBTQ individuals in Canada. The event attracted over 5,000 participants and featured a diverse lineup of speakers, including activists, artists, and community leaders. The march concluded with a rally at a central park, where participants shared personal stories of resilience and hope.

This event highlighted the importance of visibility in the fight for rights. As one speaker stated, "When we march together, we show the world that we will not be silenced." The media coverage following the event was overwhelmingly positive, helping to shift public perception and garner support for legislative changes.

Case Study 2: The Protest Against Conversion Therapy   Alec played a pivotal role in organizing a protest against conversion therapy in 2020, a practice widely discredited and condemned by medical professionals. The protest was strategically timed to coincide with a parliamentary discussion on banning the practice, thus maximizing its impact.

Participants were encouraged to share their stories of survival and resilience through art, music, and spoken word. The event was not only a protest but also a celebration of LGBTQ identities. The media coverage highlighted the emotional testimonies of survivors, contributing to a growing public outcry against conversion therapy. As a result, several provinces moved towards banning the practice, showcasing the power of organized protests in effecting change.

Conclusion

Organizing protests and demonstrations is a vital aspect of Alec Butler's activism, embodying the spirit of resistance and the pursuit of justice within the LGBTQ community. Through strategic planning, coalition-building, and effective messaging, Alec has demonstrated how grassroots efforts can lead to meaningful change. The legacy of these protests continues to inspire future generations of activists, reminding us that the fight for equality is ongoing and that every voice matters in the chorus for justice.

Influencing policy change through grassroots activism

Grassroots activism has emerged as a powerful tool for influencing policy change, particularly within marginalized communities, including the LGBTQ community. This approach emphasizes the importance of community engagement, collective action, and local leadership in advocating for rights and social justice. Alec Butler's journey in grassroots activism exemplifies how individual efforts can catalyze significant changes in public policy.

Theoretical Framework

Grassroots activism is rooted in several theoretical frameworks, including social movement theory and community organizing principles. According to Tilly and Tarrow (2015), social movements are collective challenges to elites, authorities, or cultural codes by people with common purposes and solidarity. This theory posits that grassroots movements arise from the need to address social injustices that are often overlooked by traditional political structures.

$$\text{Social Change} = f(\text{Collective Action, Community Engagement}) \qquad (7)$$

In this equation, social change is a function of collective action and community engagement, highlighting the critical role that grassroots movements play in shaping policies that affect marginalized groups.

Challenges Faced

While grassroots activism is an effective means of influencing policy change, it is not without its challenges. Activists often encounter systemic barriers, including:

- **Institutional Resistance:** Many policymakers may resist changes that threaten the status quo. This resistance can manifest in bureaucratic red tape or outright hostility towards LGBTQ rights.

- **Limited Resources:** Grassroots organizations often operate with minimal funding and manpower, making it difficult to sustain long-term campaigns.

- **Public Perception:** Misunderstanding or hostility from the broader public can hinder grassroots efforts. Activists must work to educate and engage community members to build support for their causes.

Alec Butler's Activism: A Case Study

Alec Butler's grassroots activism has been instrumental in advocating for policy changes that benefit the LGBTQ community. One notable example is Butler's involvement in organizing the "Pride for Policy" campaign, which aimed to influence local government decisions regarding LGBTQ rights.

Key Strategies Employed

1. **Community Mobilization:** Butler engaged local community members through workshops and town hall meetings, fostering a sense of solidarity and shared purpose. This mobilization was crucial in gathering support for policy initiatives.

2. **Coalition Building:** Recognizing the power of collective action, Butler collaborated with various LGBTQ organizations, Indigenous groups, and allies to amplify their voices. This coalition-building helped to create a unified front in advocating for policy reforms.

3. **Direct Action:** Butler and their allies organized peaceful protests and demonstrations to draw attention to LGBTQ issues. These actions not only

raised public awareness but also pressured policymakers to address the concerns of the community.

4. **Engaging with Policymakers:** Butler understood the importance of direct engagement with those in power. They arranged meetings with local officials to discuss policy changes, providing them with data and personal stories to illustrate the need for reform.

Successful Outcomes

The concerted efforts of grassroots activists, including Butler, led to significant policy changes, such as:

+ **Anti-Discrimination Legislation:** The campaign successfully influenced local lawmakers to pass anti-discrimination laws protecting LGBTQ individuals in housing and employment.

+ **Inclusive Education Policies:** Butler's advocacy resulted in the implementation of inclusive curricula in local schools, promoting understanding and acceptance of LGBTQ identities among students.

+ **Increased Funding for LGBTQ Services:** Through persistent lobbying, Butler helped secure additional funding for LGBTQ health services and community programs, addressing critical gaps in support.

Conclusion

Alec Butler's grassroots activism serves as a powerful reminder of the impact that community-driven efforts can have on policy change. By mobilizing individuals, building coalitions, and engaging directly with policymakers, activists can challenge systemic barriers and advocate for the rights of marginalized communities. The legacy of Butler's work highlights the importance of grassroots movements in shaping a more equitable society for all, particularly within the LGBTQ community.

As we reflect on the lessons learned from Butler's journey, it becomes clear that grassroots activism is not merely a strategy; it is a vital force for social change that empowers individuals and communities to reclaim their voices and demand justice.

The fight against discrimination

Exposing systemic LGBTQ discrimination in Canada

In the vibrant tapestry of Canadian society, the threads of systemic discrimination against the LGBTQ community are woven deeply into the fabric of its institutions, policies, and cultural narratives. Despite Canada's reputation as a progressive nation, the reality is that LGBTQ individuals, particularly those who identify as Two-Spirit, face multifaceted discrimination that manifests in various forms, including legal, social, and economic inequalities.

Understanding Systemic Discrimination

Systemic discrimination refers to the policies and practices entrenched in established institutions that disproportionately disadvantage certain groups. According to the *Canadian Human Rights Commission*, systemic discrimination can occur even without overtly discriminatory intent. It is often perpetuated by societal norms and practices that favor the majority, creating barriers for marginalized groups.

For the LGBTQ community, these barriers can be seen in several critical areas:

+ **Employment Discrimination:** Many LGBTQ individuals report facing discrimination during hiring processes, leading to higher unemployment rates compared to their heterosexual counterparts. A survey conducted by *Statistics Canada* found that LGBTQ individuals experience higher levels of job insecurity and lower wages, which can be attributed to both overt discrimination and subtle biases in workplace cultures.

+ **Healthcare Inequities:** Access to healthcare is another area where systemic discrimination is prevalent. Studies have shown that LGBTQ individuals often face discrimination from healthcare providers, leading to reluctance in seeking medical care. The *Canadian LGBTQ Health Survey* revealed that 30% of LGBTQ respondents had experienced discrimination in healthcare settings, impacting their overall health and well-being.

+ **Educational Barriers:** LGBTQ youth face significant challenges within educational institutions, including bullying and harassment, which can lead to higher dropout rates. The *Youth Risk Behavior Survey* indicates that LGBTQ students are more likely to experience violence and discrimination, affecting their academic performance and mental health.

+ **Legal Inequalities:** While Canada has made strides in legal recognition of LGBTQ rights, there remain gaps in protections, particularly for Two-Spirit and Indigenous LGBTQ individuals. The lack of comprehensive anti-discrimination legislation at the provincial level means that many LGBTQ individuals can still be legally discriminated against in housing, employment, and public services.

Theoretical Perspectives on Discrimination

To understand the systemic nature of LGBTQ discrimination, several theoretical frameworks can be applied:

+ **Intersectionality:** Coined by Kimberlé Crenshaw, the concept of intersectionality is crucial in examining how various forms of discrimination overlap. Two-Spirit individuals, for instance, experience a unique intersection of gender identity, sexual orientation, and Indigenous identity, which compounds their experiences of discrimination. This framework helps to highlight the need for nuanced approaches in addressing the specific needs of marginalized groups within the LGBTQ community.

+ **Critical Queer Theory:** This theory challenges the binary understanding of gender and sexuality, advocating for a more inclusive framework that recognizes the fluidity of identities. It posits that societal norms are constructed and maintained through power dynamics that marginalize non-heteronormative identities. By applying critical queer theory, activists like Alec Butler can expose the limitations of current policies and advocate for broader recognition of diverse identities.

+ **Social Justice Framework:** This framework emphasizes the importance of equity and fairness in social policies. By advocating for systemic change, activists can work towards dismantling the structures that perpetuate discrimination. This involves not just addressing individual acts of discrimination, but also challenging the policies and practices that sustain systemic inequalities.

Case Studies and Examples

Several case studies exemplify the systemic discrimination faced by the LGBTQ community in Canada:

- **The Toronto Police Service:** In recent years, the Toronto Police Service has faced criticism for its treatment of LGBTQ individuals, particularly during the 2016 Pride parade when officers were barred from marching in uniform. This incident highlighted the ongoing tensions between law enforcement and the LGBTQ community, raising questions about safety and trust in policing. Activists have called for reforms to ensure that police practices are more inclusive and sensitive to LGBTQ issues.

- **Transgender Rights in Healthcare:** The exclusion of gender-affirming surgeries from provincial healthcare plans has been a significant issue for many transgender individuals. In 2019, a landmark decision in British Columbia mandated that the province must provide coverage for gender-affirming surgeries, yet many provinces still lag behind. This inconsistency in healthcare access illustrates the systemic barriers that transgender individuals face across different regions.

- **Two-Spirit Youth and Education:** A 2020 report from the *Canadian Teachers' Federation* highlighted the challenges faced by Two-Spirit youth in educational settings, including high rates of bullying and a lack of representation in curricula. This report emphasized the need for schools to create inclusive environments that recognize and celebrate Two-Spirit identities, thereby addressing the systemic barriers that hinder their educational success.

Activism and Advocacy Against Discrimination

Activists like Alec Butler have played a pivotal role in exposing and combating systemic discrimination against LGBTQ individuals in Canada. Through public speaking, art, and community organizing, they have brought attention to the injustices faced by marginalized groups.

- **Grassroots Movements:** Organizations such as *Pride Toronto* and *The 519* have been at the forefront of advocacy efforts, mobilizing communities to challenge discriminatory practices and policies. These organizations work to provide resources, support, and safe spaces for LGBTQ individuals, particularly those from marginalized backgrounds.

- **Policy Change Initiatives:** By collaborating with policymakers and engaging in advocacy campaigns, activists have sought to influence legislation that impacts LGBTQ rights. The push for comprehensive anti-discrimination laws reflects a broader movement towards ensuring equality for all individuals, regardless of sexual orientation or gender identity.

⋆ **Cultural Representation:** The importance of visibility cannot be overstated. By amplifying LGBTQ voices in media, art, and literature, activists are challenging stereotypes and fostering a more inclusive narrative that reflects the diversity of the LGBTQ experience. This representation is crucial in combating systemic discrimination and promoting acceptance within society.

Conclusion

Exposing systemic LGBTQ discrimination in Canada requires a multi-faceted approach that acknowledges the complexities of identity and the pervasive nature of bias within societal structures. Through activism, advocacy, and education, individuals like Alec Butler are challenging the status quo and working towards a more equitable society for all. It is essential to continue this fight, as the journey towards equality is ongoing, and the voices of those affected by discrimination must remain at the forefront of the conversation.

Advocating for equal rights and protections

In the vibrant tapestry of LGBTQ activism, advocating for equal rights and protections stands as a cornerstone of Alec Butler's mission. This advocacy is not merely a political endeavor; it is a deeply personal journey rooted in the lived experiences of countless individuals who have faced discrimination, marginalization, and violence. The struggle for equal rights is a multifaceted issue that intersects with various aspects of society, including law, culture, and identity.

Theoretical Framework

To understand the importance of advocating for equal rights, one must consider the theoretical frameworks that underpin LGBTQ activism. The *Queer Theory*, for instance, challenges normative assumptions about gender and sexuality, advocating for a society that embraces diversity in all its forms. This theoretical perspective asserts that identity is fluid and that societal norms should evolve to reflect this complexity.

Additionally, the *Intersectionality Theory*, coined by Kimberlé Crenshaw, highlights how various forms of identity—such as race, gender, and sexual orientation—intersect to create unique experiences of oppression and privilege.

For Two-Spirit individuals like Alec, this intersectionality is crucial, as it underscores the need for a holistic approach to advocacy that addresses the specific challenges faced by Indigenous LGBTQ individuals.

Challenges in the Fight for Equality

Despite significant progress in recent years, advocating for equal rights and protections remains fraught with challenges. Discrimination against LGBTQ individuals persists in many areas, including employment, healthcare, and housing. For instance, a 2019 survey by the Canadian LGBTQ+ Survey revealed that 25% of LGBTQ individuals experienced discrimination in the workplace due to their sexual orientation or gender identity. This statistic underscores the systemic nature of discrimination, necessitating a robust response from activists and allies alike.

Moreover, the legal landscape for LGBTQ rights is uneven across Canada. While same-sex marriage was legalized nationwide in 2005, many provinces lack comprehensive anti-discrimination laws that explicitly protect LGBTQ individuals. This patchwork of legal protections creates vulnerabilities for marginalized groups, making advocacy for equal rights a pressing issue.

Examples of Advocacy Efforts

Alec Butler's advocacy efforts exemplify the power of grassroots movements in pushing for equal rights. One notable initiative was the organization of the *Pride in Politics* campaign, which aimed to increase LGBTQ representation in political offices across Canada. By collaborating with local LGBTQ organizations, Alec mobilized community members to participate in political processes, emphasizing the importance of representation in enacting change.

In addition to political engagement, Alec has utilized artistic expression as a means of advocacy. Through powerful performances and art installations, they have addressed themes of discrimination and resilience, fostering dialogue around LGBTQ rights. For instance, Alec's piece titled *Unfiltered Voices* showcased the stories of LGBTQ individuals who have faced discrimination, highlighting the need for systemic change and greater protections.

Legislative Advocacy and Policy Change

Advocating for equal rights also involves engaging with policymakers to enact legislative changes. Alec has been instrumental in lobbying for the implementation of comprehensive anti-discrimination laws at both the provincial and federal levels. Their efforts contributed to the introduction of the *LGBTQ+ Rights Protection*

Act, which aimed to expand protections for LGBTQ individuals in employment, housing, and public services.

Furthermore, Alec has participated in various public speaking engagements, where they have shared their personal experiences and the stories of others to humanize the issues at stake. By appealing to the empathy of lawmakers and the general public, Alec's advocacy has helped to shift perceptions and galvanize support for LGBTQ rights.

The Role of Allies in Advocacy

While individual activism is vital, the role of allies in advocating for equal rights cannot be overstated. Allies play a crucial role in amplifying the voices of marginalized communities and challenging discriminatory practices within their spheres of influence. Alec has consistently emphasized the importance of allyship in their advocacy work, encouraging individuals to educate themselves about LGBTQ issues and to stand in solidarity with the community.

In conclusion, advocating for equal rights and protections is an ongoing struggle that requires a multifaceted approach. Through theoretical frameworks, addressing systemic challenges, and engaging in both grassroots and legislative efforts, activists like Alec Butler continue to pave the way for a more equitable society. The journey is far from over, but the commitment to fighting for equal rights remains steadfast, fueled by the belief that everyone deserves to live authentically and without fear of discrimination.

Confronting homophobia and transphobia in society

Homophobia and transphobia are pervasive issues that infiltrate various aspects of society, creating a climate of fear and discrimination for LGBTQ individuals. To confront these societal challenges, activists like Alec Butler have employed a multi-faceted approach that encompasses education, advocacy, and community engagement.

Understanding Homophobia and Transphobia

Homophobia refers to the irrational fear or hatred of individuals who identify as gay, lesbian, or bisexual, while transphobia encompasses similar sentiments directed towards transgender individuals. These prejudices are not merely personal biases; they are embedded within societal structures and cultural narratives, leading to systemic discrimination. Theories such as Social Identity Theory suggest that individuals derive part of their self-concept from their group memberships, which can lead to in-group favoritism and out-group discrimination. This theory helps explain why some individuals may feel threatened by those who identify outside of traditional gender and sexual norms.

The Impact of Homophobia and Transphobia

The consequences of homophobia and transphobia are severe and far-reaching. LGBTQ individuals often experience higher rates of mental health issues, including depression and anxiety, as a result of societal rejection and discrimination. According to a study published in the *American Journal of Public Health*, LGBTQ youth are significantly more likely to experience suicidal ideation compared to their heterosexual peers. This alarming statistic underscores the urgency of addressing these prejudices.

Activism and Advocacy Strategies

Alec Butler's activism has focused on dismantling these harmful attitudes through various strategies:

- **Education and Awareness Campaigns:** By organizing workshops and community discussions, activists aim to educate the public about LGBTQ issues, fostering empathy and understanding. For instance, Butler has collaborated with local schools to implement educational programs that address the history and rights of LGBTQ individuals, thus challenging stereotypes and misinformation.

- **Art as a Medium for Change:** Butler has utilized performance art as a powerful tool for confronting societal norms. Through provocative performances that highlight the struggles faced by LGBTQ individuals, Butler not only entertains but also educates audiences, prompting them to reflect on their own biases. The integration of personal narratives in art can humanize the experiences of marginalized groups, making it harder for audiences to maintain prejudiced views.

- **Public Speaking and Media Engagement:** By sharing their story through public speaking engagements, Butler has reached diverse audiences, including policymakers and community leaders. This visibility is crucial in challenging misconceptions and advocating for policy changes that protect LGBTQ rights. For example, Butler's testimony at a provincial hearing on anti-discrimination laws helped to influence legislative reforms.

+ **Community Building:** Creating safe spaces for LGBTQ individuals fosters a sense of belonging and empowerment. Butler has been instrumental in establishing community centers that provide resources and support for LGBTQ youth, helping to combat the isolation often felt by those facing discrimination.

Confronting Systemic Issues

To effectively confront homophobia and transphobia, it is essential to address the systemic issues that perpetuate these biases. This includes advocating for comprehensive anti-discrimination laws that protect LGBTQ individuals in employment, housing, and healthcare. Activists like Butler have worked tirelessly to influence policy changes at both local and national levels, emphasizing the need for legal protections that reflect the dignity and rights of all individuals, regardless of their sexual orientation or gender identity.

Examples of Successful Initiatives

Several successful initiatives have emerged from Butler's activism, exemplifying the potential for change. One notable example is the "Pride in the Park" event, which Butler organized to celebrate LGBTQ identities while also addressing issues of discrimination. This event not only provided a platform for LGBTQ artists and speakers but also attracted allies from various backgrounds, fostering a sense of solidarity and community.

Additionally, Butler's collaboration with Indigenous activists to promote Two-Spirit visibility has been crucial in confronting both homophobia and colonial legacies that marginalize Indigenous LGBTQ individuals. This intersectional approach highlights the importance of acknowledging diverse identities within the broader LGBTQ movement.

Conclusion

Confronting homophobia and transphobia requires a collective effort that encompasses education, advocacy, and community engagement. Activists like Alec Butler exemplify the power of resilience and creativity in the face of discrimination, demonstrating that change is possible when individuals unite to challenge societal norms. By fostering dialogue, promoting understanding, and advocating for systemic change, we can create a more inclusive society where all individuals are free to express their identities without fear of prejudice.

Engaging with policymakers to create change

Engaging with policymakers is a critical component of advocacy for LGBTQ rights, especially for marginalized voices such as Two-Spirit individuals. This section explores the theoretical frameworks, challenges, and practical examples of effective engagement strategies that activists like Alec Butler have employed to influence policy change.

Theoretical Frameworks

The engagement of policymakers can be understood through various theoretical lenses, including the Advocacy Coalition Framework (ACF) and the Multiple Streams Framework (MSF).

Advocacy Coalition Framework The ACF posits that policy change occurs through the collaboration of various stakeholders who share a common belief system.   In the context of LGBTQ rights, coalitions may include activists, community organizations, and sympathetic policymakers who work together to influence legislative outcomes.   According to Sabatier (1988), "The key to understanding policy change is to analyze the interactions of advocacy coalitions."

Multiple Streams Framework The MSF, developed by Kingdon (1995), suggests that policy change occurs when three streams—problems, policies, and politics—converge.   For LGBTQ activists, identifying a pressing problem (e.g., discrimination against Two-Spirit individuals), proposing viable policy solutions (e.g., anti-discrimination laws), and leveraging political opportunities (e.g., a sympathetic government) are crucial for successful engagement.

Challenges in Engagement

Despite the theoretical frameworks available, engaging with policymakers presents significant challenges:

1. Systemic Barriers Many LGBTQ activists face systemic barriers that hinder their ability to engage effectively with policymakers. These barriers can include a lack of representation in political spaces, insufficient resources for advocacy, and entrenched biases within governmental structures.

2. Misunderstanding of LGBTQ Issues   Policymakers may not fully understand the complexities of LGBTQ issues, particularly those related to Two-Spirit identities. This lack of understanding can lead to inadequate policies that fail to address the needs of marginalized communities.

3. Political Polarization   The increasing polarization of political environments can create hostile atmospheres for LGBTQ advocacy. Activists may encounter resistance from policymakers who hold anti-LGBTQ sentiments, making it difficult to advance their agendas.

Strategies for Effective Engagement

To overcome these challenges, activists like Alec Butler have developed several strategies for engaging with policymakers:

1. Building Relationships   Establishing strong relationships with policymakers is essential for effective advocacy. This can involve regular communication, attending town hall meetings, and inviting policymakers to community events. By fostering personal connections, activists can create a sense of trust and understanding.

2. Providing Education and Resources   Activists can engage with policymakers by providing educational resources that clarify LGBTQ issues and their implications for public policy. This may include fact sheets, research studies, and personal testimonies from affected individuals. For example, Alec Butler might present data illustrating the disproportionate rates of violence faced by Two-Spirit individuals, thereby emphasizing the need for targeted policy interventions.

3. Mobilizing Community Support   Activists can leverage community support to amplify their voices when engaging with policymakers. Organizing rallies, letter-writing campaigns, and social media initiatives can demonstrate public demand for change. For instance, a well-coordinated campaign that highlights the need for inclusive policies may encourage policymakers to prioritize LGBTQ rights.

4. Utilizing Media Platforms   Media engagement is a powerful tool for influencing policymakers. Activists can utilize traditional and social media to raise awareness about LGBTQ issues, thereby putting pressure on policymakers to respond. For example, Alec Butler could use social media platforms to share stories of Two-Spirit individuals, creating a narrative that compels policymakers to take action.

Examples of Successful Engagement

Several examples illustrate the successful engagement of policymakers by LGBTQ activists:

1. The Ontario Human Rights Code   In 2012, LGBTQ activists, including Alec Butler, successfully lobbied for amendments to the Ontario Human Rights Code to include gender identity and expression as protected grounds. This victory was the result of sustained advocacy efforts, including community mobilization and strategic engagement with sympathetic lawmakers.

2. The Federal Bill C-16   The passage of Bill C-16 in Canada, which added gender identity and expression to the list of prohibited grounds of discrimination, was significantly influenced by grassroots activism.   Activists engaged with policymakers through public consultations, providing testimony that highlighted the urgent need for legal protections for transgender and Two-Spirit individuals.

3. The 2SLGBTQ+ Youth Strategy   The Canadian government's 2SLGBTQ+ Youth Strategy was developed in response to advocacy from LGBTQ organizations and youth. Activists engaged with policymakers through consultations, sharing the unique challenges faced by Two-Spirit youth and advocating for resources to support their well-being.

Conclusion

Engaging with policymakers is a vital strategy for LGBTQ activists seeking to create meaningful change. By employing theoretical frameworks to understand the policy landscape, overcoming challenges through strategic engagement, and learning from successful examples, activists like Alec Butler can continue to advocate for the rights and recognition of Two-Spirit individuals. The need for unfiltered voices in these discussions cannot be overstated, as they bring authenticity and urgency to the fight for equality.

$$\text{Policy Change} = f(\text{Coalition Building, Education, Community Support, Media Engage}$$
$$(8)$$

Two-Spirit empowerment

Embracing Two-Spirit identity

The meaning and significance of Two-Spirit

The term *Two-Spirit* is a contemporary, pan-Indigenous term that encapsulates a range of gender identities and sexual orientations within Indigenous cultures. It emerged in the 1990s as a way to provide a unifying term for Indigenous peoples who embody both masculine and feminine spirits, thereby challenging the binary gender norms prevalent in Western societies. The significance of Two-Spirit identity is deeply rooted in Indigenous cosmologies, which often recognize multiple gender roles and fluidity in gender expression.

Cultural Context

Historically, many Indigenous cultures in North America recognized and honored individuals who were seen as embodying both male and female qualities. These individuals often held special societal roles, such as healers, mediators, or spiritual leaders. For example, the *Nadleeh* of the Navajo Nation and the *Berdache* in various Plains tribes were revered for their unique perspectives and abilities to bridge gender divides. The Two-Spirit identity is not merely an LGBTQ identity; it is a reclamation of Indigenous cultural practices and a resistance against colonial narratives that sought to erase these identities.

Theoretical Framework

From a theoretical standpoint, Two-Spirit identity can be analyzed through the lens of intersectionality, a framework developed by Kimberlé Crenshaw that examines how various social identities intersect to create unique modes of discrimination and privilege. Two-Spirit individuals often navigate multiple layers of identity, including their Indigenous heritage, gender identity, and sexual orientation. This intersectional approach allows for a nuanced understanding of the challenges faced by Two-Spirit people, including discrimination from both Indigenous and non-Indigenous communities.

The equation for understanding intersectionality can be expressed as follows:

$$I = G + S + C \tag{9}$$

Where:

+ I represents the individual's identity,

+ G is their gender identity,

+ S is their sexual orientation,

+ C denotes their cultural background.

This equation illustrates that identity is not singular but a complex interplay of various factors that shape an individual's lived experience.

Challenges Faced by Two-Spirit Individuals

Despite the rich cultural heritage associated with Two-Spirit identities, contemporary Two-Spirit individuals face numerous challenges. The legacy of colonialism has resulted in systemic discrimination, marginalization, and violence against Indigenous peoples, which disproportionately affects Two-Spirit individuals. Many experience a disconnection from their cultural roots due to historical trauma, and this disconnection can lead to issues such as mental health struggles, substance abuse, and homelessness.

Moreover, Two-Spirit individuals often find themselves at the intersection of LGBTQ and Indigenous rights movements, sometimes facing exclusion from both. This marginalization can create a sense of isolation, making it imperative for advocacy efforts to address the unique needs of Two-Spirit people.

Examples of Two-Spirit Empowerment

In recent years, there has been a resurgence of interest in Two-Spirit identities within Indigenous communities. Events such as Two-Spirit powwows and gatherings have emerged as platforms for celebration and empowerment. These gatherings provide safe spaces for Two-Spirit individuals to express their identities openly and connect with others who share similar experiences.

One notable example is the work of the *Two-Spirit Gathering* held annually in various locations across North America, where Two-Spirit individuals and allies come together to share stories, art, and cultural practices. Such events foster community, resilience, and healing, reinforcing the significance of Two-Spirit identities within both Indigenous and LGBTQ contexts.

Conclusion

In conclusion, the meaning and significance of Two-Spirit identity extend far beyond a simple label. It is a rich tapestry woven from the threads of culture, history, and identity, representing a profound understanding of gender and sexuality that challenges Western binaries. As society continues to evolve, embracing the complexities of identity, the Two-Spirit movement stands as a powerful testament to resilience, cultural reclamation, and the ongoing fight for recognition and respect within both Indigenous and LGBTQ communities.

The journey of Two-Spirit individuals is one of empowerment, and their voices are crucial in shaping a more inclusive future that honors diversity in all its forms.

Challenging traditional gender norms within Indigenous communities

In the tapestry of Indigenous cultures, gender has often been understood through a lens that transcends the binary constructs prevalent in Western societies. The concept of Two-Spirit, which encompasses a spectrum of gender identities and expressions, has historically existed within many Indigenous cultures. However, the imposition of colonial ideologies has led to a profound disruption of these traditional understandings. This section explores how Alec Butler, as a Two-Spirit activist, challenges the restrictive gender norms that have been enforced within Indigenous communities and advocates for a reclamation of indigenous gender identities.

Historical Context and Colonial Impact

The arrival of European colonizers brought with it rigid gender binaries that often disregarded the fluidity of gender roles present in Indigenous cultures. Many Indigenous communities recognized and revered individuals who embodied both masculine and feminine traits, viewing them as possessing unique spiritual gifts. The term "Two-Spirit" itself is a contemporary label that reflects a range of identities historically recognized by Indigenous peoples, encompassing both gender and sexual diversity.

However, colonial policies aimed at eradicating Indigenous cultures systematically undermined these identities. The Indian Act, established in Canada in 1876, imposed Western definitions of gender and sexuality, leading to the marginalization of Two-Spirit individuals. This historical context is crucial for understanding the contemporary struggles faced by Two-Spirit people within Indigenous communities.

Reclaiming Identity and Cultural Heritage

Alec Butler's activism is deeply rooted in the reclamation of Two-Spirit identities as a means of resisting colonial narratives. By advocating for the visibility of Two-Spirit individuals, Butler seeks to dismantle the stigma associated with non-binary and gender-fluid identities. This reclamation is not merely a personal journey; it is a collective movement that calls for a return to traditional understandings of gender within Indigenous communities.

One powerful example of this reclamation can be seen in cultural events and gatherings that celebrate Two-Spirit identities. These events often include storytelling, art, and performance, allowing Two-Spirit individuals to express their identities authentically. Such spaces foster a sense of belonging and empower individuals to embrace their unique contributions to their communities.

Challenging Internalized Norms

While the impact of colonialism is evident, it is also essential to recognize the internalized gender norms that persist within some Indigenous communities. Many Two-Spirit individuals face discrimination not only from outside their communities but also from within. This internalized prejudice can manifest in the form of exclusion from cultural practices, community events, or even family structures.

Butler's activism addresses these challenges head-on by promoting dialogue and education within Indigenous communities. Workshops, community forums, and artistic expressions serve as platforms for discussing the importance of embracing diverse gender identities. By sharing personal narratives and experiences, Butler and other activists challenge the misconceptions surrounding Two-Spirit identities, fostering a more inclusive understanding within their communities.

Intersectionality and Inclusivity

A critical aspect of challenging traditional gender norms is recognizing the intersectionality of identities. Two-Spirit individuals often navigate multiple layers of identity, including ethnicity, sexual orientation, and socio-economic status. Butler emphasizes the importance of inclusivity within the LGBTQ movement, advocating for a broader understanding of how these intersecting identities shape the experiences of Two-Spirit people.

By collaborating with Indigenous activists and organizations, Butler seeks to create a unified front that addresses the unique challenges faced by Two-Spirit individuals. This collaboration not only strengthens the fight against discrimination but also enriches the broader LGBTQ movement by incorporating Indigenous perspectives and experiences.

Conclusion

Challenging traditional gender norms within Indigenous communities is a complex and multifaceted endeavor. Alec Butler's activism serves as a beacon of hope for Two-Spirit individuals seeking to reclaim their identities and navigate the legacies of colonialism. By fostering dialogue, promoting visibility, and advocating for inclusivity, Butler and other activists are paving the way for a future where diverse gender identities are celebrated and honored within Indigenous cultures. In doing so, they are not only challenging the status quo but also revitalizing the rich tapestry of Indigenous gender identities that has endured despite centuries of oppression.

$$\text{Visibility} + \text{Education} + \text{Inclusivity} = \text{Empowerment} \qquad (10)$$

As this equation illustrates, the combination of visibility, education, and inclusivity is essential for empowering Two-Spirit individuals and dismantling the barriers imposed by traditional gender norms. The journey towards acceptance and understanding is ongoing, but with the efforts of activists like Alec Butler, the future holds promise for a more inclusive and equitable society.

Empowering Two-Spirit individuals through visibility and representation

The empowerment of Two-Spirit individuals is intricately linked to the visibility and representation of their identities within both Indigenous and broader LGBTQ communities. Visibility serves as a powerful tool in combating stereotypes, fostering acceptance, and promoting a deeper understanding of the diverse spectrum of gender identities. The term "Two-Spirit" itself, which encompasses a range of gender identities and expressions in Indigenous cultures, signifies a unique cultural perspective that challenges the binary notions prevalent in Western societies.

Theoretical Framework

The theoretical framework surrounding visibility and representation can be understood through various lenses, including queer theory and intersectionality. Queer theory, as posited by scholars such as Judith Butler and Eve Kosofsky Sedgwick, suggests that identity is not fixed but rather fluid and socially constructed. This perspective allows for a broader understanding of Two-Spirit identities, which often transcend conventional gender categories. Intersectionality, introduced by Kimberlé Crenshaw, highlights the interconnected nature of social categorizations such as race, gender, and sexuality, and how they create overlapping systems of discrimination or disadvantage. This is particularly relevant for Two-Spirit individuals, who navigate both Indigenous and LGBTQ identities, often facing unique challenges that require nuanced approaches to advocacy and representation.

Challenges of Visibility

Despite the importance of visibility, Two-Spirit individuals often encounter significant barriers that hinder their representation. One major challenge is the historical erasure of Two-Spirit identities within both Indigenous and non-Indigenous contexts. Colonialism has led to the marginalization of Indigenous cultures and their gender diversity, resulting in a lack of acknowledgment and understanding of Two-Spirit identities. Furthermore, mainstream LGBTQ movements have, at times, overlooked the specific needs and experiences of Two-Spirit individuals, perpetuating a sense of invisibility within both communities.

Additionally, the stigma associated with being LGBTQ in many Indigenous communities can lead to internalized homophobia and fear of rejection. This can create a reluctance among Two-Spirit individuals to express their identities openly, further perpetuating cycles of invisibility. The lack of representation in media, educational institutions, and public discourse exacerbates these issues, leaving Two-Spirit voices unheard and unrecognized.

Examples of Empowerment through Representation

Empowering Two-Spirit individuals through visibility and representation can take many forms. One notable example is the work of Two-Spirit artists and activists who use their platforms to share their stories and challenge societal norms. For instance, the art of Two-Spirit creator *[insert name here]* has garnered attention for its bold exploration of identity and cultural heritage. Their exhibitions not only celebrate Two-Spirit identity but also educate audiences about the rich history and significance of gender diversity within Indigenous cultures.

Moreover, initiatives such as the Two-Spirit Pride events across Canada provide spaces for celebration and affirmation of Two-Spirit identities. These events foster community, create opportunities for networking, and promote visibility in a society that often marginalizes Indigenous voices. By organizing such events, Two-Spirit activists are reclaiming their narratives and asserting their place within both Indigenous and LGBTQ communities.

The Role of Media and Representation

The media plays a crucial role in shaping public perceptions of Two-Spirit individuals. Positive representation in film, television, and literature can challenge stereotypes and foster a greater understanding of Two-Spirit identities. For example, the inclusion of Two-Spirit characters in popular television shows has sparked conversations about gender diversity and representation. By portraying nuanced and authentic Two-Spirit experiences, media can help dismantle harmful stereotypes and promote acceptance.

Additionally, social media platforms have become vital spaces for Two-Spirit individuals to share their stories and connect with others. Hashtags such as #TwoSpirit and #TwoSpiritPride have emerged as rallying points for visibility, allowing individuals to showcase their identities and advocate for their rights. This digital activism not only empowers Two-Spirit individuals but also educates allies and the broader public about the importance of representation.

Conclusion

In conclusion, empowering Two-Spirit individuals through visibility and representation is essential for fostering acceptance, challenging stereotypes, and promoting understanding of diverse gender identities. By addressing the challenges of invisibility and advocating for authentic representation in various spheres, we can create a more inclusive society that honors and celebrates the richness of Two-Spirit identities. As we continue to amplify Two-Spirit voices, we pave the way for future generations to embrace their identities with pride and confidence, ensuring that the legacy of Two-Spirit empowerment endures.

Collaboration with Indigenous activists and organizations

The journey of Alec Butler as a Two-Spirit activist is deeply intertwined with the rich tapestry of Indigenous culture and community. Recognizing the historical and ongoing struggles faced by Indigenous peoples, Alec has dedicated a significant portion of their advocacy to collaborating with Indigenous activists and organizations. This collaboration is not merely an act of solidarity but a profound acknowledgment of the shared histories and interconnected struggles for rights, recognition, and respect.

Understanding Two-Spirit Identity

The term "Two-Spirit" is a contemporary umbrella term used by some Indigenous North Americans to describe a person who embodies both masculine and feminine spirits. This identity is rooted in Indigenous cultural traditions and spiritual beliefs, which often recognize multiple gender identities beyond the binary framework imposed by colonialism. Alec's collaboration with Indigenous activists emphasizes the importance of reclaiming and celebrating Two-Spirit identities within the broader LGBTQ movement.

Theoretical Framework

Collaboration between LGBTQ activists and Indigenous organizations can be understood through the lens of intersectionality, a concept coined by Kimberlé Crenshaw. Intersectionality posits that individuals experience multiple, overlapping identities that can lead to unique experiences of oppression and privilege. For Two-Spirit individuals, this means navigating both the challenges of being LGBTQ and the historical trauma associated with colonialism and Indigenous erasure. By embracing an intersectional approach, Alec and their collaborators work to dismantle the systems of oppression that affect both communities.

Challenges in Collaboration

Despite the shared goals of LGBTQ and Indigenous activists, collaboration is not without its challenges. One significant issue is the historical mistrust that exists between Indigenous peoples and non-Indigenous LGBTQ activists. This mistrust stems from a long history of colonial violence, cultural appropriation, and the marginalization of Indigenous voices within the LGBTQ movement. Alec recognizes that building trust requires active listening, humility, and a commitment to amplifying Indigenous voices in all discussions and initiatives.

Another challenge lies in the differing priorities and approaches to activism. While LGBTQ activism may often focus on legal recognition and rights, Indigenous activism frequently centers on land rights, sovereignty, and cultural preservation. Alec has worked diligently to bridge these gaps by promoting a holistic understanding of justice that encompasses both LGBTQ rights and Indigenous rights, advocating for a unified front in the fight against oppression.

Examples of Collaboration

Alec's collaboration with Indigenous activists has taken many forms, including joint protests, community workshops, and public speaking engagements. One notable example is their participation in the annual Pride celebrations in cities across Canada, where they have worked alongside Indigenous leaders to highlight the importance of recognizing Two-Spirit identities within the larger LGBTQ narrative. These events serve as a platform for educating attendees about the unique challenges faced by Two-Spirit individuals and the need for solidarity among marginalized communities.

Additionally, Alec has been involved in creating art and performance pieces that celebrate Indigenous culture while addressing LGBTQ issues. By collaborating with Indigenous artists, they have produced works that challenge stereotypes, promote understanding, and foster dialogue between different communities. One such performance piece, titled "Spirit of the Land," combines traditional Indigenous storytelling with contemporary dance, illustrating the interconnectedness of identity, culture, and activism.

Conclusion

In conclusion, Alec Butler's collaboration with Indigenous activists and organizations is a vital aspect of their work as a Two-Spirit advocate. By embracing intersectionality, addressing challenges head-on, and creating meaningful partnerships, Alec is helping to pave the way for a more inclusive and equitable future for all marginalized communities. Their efforts serve as a powerful reminder of the importance of uniting diverse voices in the ongoing struggle for justice and equality.

Building bridges between communities

Advocating for intersectionality within the LGBTQ movement

In recent years, the concept of intersectionality has emerged as a critical framework within social justice movements, including the LGBTQ movement. Coined by legal scholar Kimberlé Crenshaw in 1989, intersectionality refers to the ways in which various forms of social stratification, such as race, gender, sexual orientation, class, and disability, intersect to create unique dynamics of oppression and privilege. This theoretical framework is essential for understanding the multifaceted experiences of LGBTQ individuals, particularly those who identify with multiple marginalized identities.

Understanding Intersectionality

Intersectionality posits that individuals do not experience discrimination or privilege in isolation; rather, their identities overlap and interact in complex ways that shape their lived experiences. For example, a Black transgender woman may face discrimination not only for her gender identity but also for her race, creating a unique set of challenges that differ from those experienced by a white gay man. Thus, to advocate effectively for LGBTQ rights, activists must consider the intersectional identities of individuals within the community.

The Problems of a Non-Intersectional Approach

Historically, the LGBTQ movement has often centered on the experiences of white, cisgender, middle-class gay men, leading to the marginalization of voices from other communities. This lack of intersectionality can result in policies and advocacy efforts that fail to address the specific needs of diverse populations within the LGBTQ community. For instance, issues such as police violence disproportionately affect LGBTQ people of color, yet these experiences are often overlooked in broader LGBTQ advocacy. The absence of intersectional analysis can perpetuate systemic inequalities and alienate those who do not fit the dominant narrative.

Examples of Intersectional Advocacy

1. **Coalition Building**: Effective intersectional advocacy involves building coalitions among various marginalized groups. Organizations such as the *Black LGBTQ+ Coalition* work to amplify the voices of Black LGBTQ individuals,

ensuring their experiences and needs are prioritized in advocacy efforts. These coalitions can help foster solidarity among diverse communities, creating a more inclusive movement.

2. **Policy Development**: Intersectional advocacy also requires the development of policies that address the specific needs of diverse groups. For example, the *Transgender Day of Remembrance* not only honors the lives lost to anti-trans violence but also highlights the disproportionate impact of such violence on transgender people of color. By focusing on these intersections, advocates can push for more comprehensive protections that address the root causes of violence and discrimination.

3. **Education and Awareness**: Raising awareness about intersectionality within the LGBTQ movement is crucial. Workshops and training sessions that educate activists about the importance of intersectionality can help shift the narrative and encourage more inclusive practices. For instance, organizations like *GLAAD* have implemented training programs aimed at increasing understanding of intersectional issues among media professionals, ensuring that diverse LGBTQ voices are represented accurately and respectfully.

Challenges to Intersectional Advocacy

While advocating for intersectionality is essential, it is not without its challenges. One major hurdle is the resistance from within the LGBTQ movement itself. Some individuals may feel threatened by the inclusion of intersectional perspectives, viewing them as a dilution of the movement's focus on sexual orientation and gender identity. Additionally, resource allocation can become a contentious issue, with debates over funding and support for various intersectional initiatives.

Furthermore, intersectional advocacy requires a commitment to ongoing education and self-reflection among activists. It is crucial for allies to recognize their own privileges and biases, actively working to dismantle systems of oppression within their own communities. This self-awareness can be uncomfortable but is necessary for fostering an inclusive environment.

Conclusion

Advocating for intersectionality within the LGBTQ movement is not just a theoretical endeavor; it is a necessary practice for achieving true equality and justice. By recognizing and addressing the unique challenges faced by individuals at the intersections of multiple marginalized identities, activists can create a more inclusive and effective movement. As Alec Butler exemplifies through their work, embracing intersectionality not only strengthens the LGBTQ movement but also fosters a sense of unity and solidarity among all marginalized communities. In a world where voices are often silenced, advocating for intersectionality is a powerful act of resistance and empowerment.

Encouraging dialogue and understanding between different cultural communities

In the vibrant tapestry of the LGBTQ movement, fostering dialogue and understanding between various cultural communities is not just an aspiration; it is an imperative. Alec Butler's advocacy is rooted in the belief that intersectionality is the key to dismantling systemic oppression and creating a united front for all marginalized identities. This section explores the theoretical foundations, challenges, and practical examples of building bridges between diverse cultural communities within the LGBTQ spectrum.

Theoretical Foundations

The concept of *intersectionality*, coined by Kimberlé Crenshaw, serves as a foundational theory for understanding how different social identities—such as race, gender, sexuality, and class—intersect to create unique experiences of oppression and privilege. Intersectionality posits that individuals do not experience discrimination in isolation; rather, their identities are interconnected, leading to multifaceted experiences that must be acknowledged in advocacy efforts.

Mathematically, we can represent the complexity of intersectionality through a simple model:

$$E = f(I_1, I_2, I_3, \ldots, I_n) \tag{11}$$

where E represents the experience of an individual, and $I_1, I_2, I_3, \ldots, I_n$ represent various intersecting identities (e.g., race, sexual orientation, gender identity). This equation illustrates that the experience of oppression or privilege is a function of multiple identities, necessitating a dialogue that encompasses all aspects of a person's identity.

Challenges to Dialogue

Despite the theoretical underpinnings, encouraging dialogue between cultural communities is fraught with challenges. One significant barrier is the tendency for communities to prioritize their specific issues over collective concerns. For instance, an LGBTQ group may focus on same-sex marriage rights, while Indigenous Two-Spirit individuals might emphasize the need for recognition of their unique cultural heritage and rights. This divergence can lead to fragmentation, where communities fail to support one another, ultimately weakening the collective struggle for equality.

Moreover, historical tensions and mistrust between cultural groups can hinder open dialogue. For example, the legacy of colonialism has created rifts between Indigenous communities and settler populations, which can extend into the LGBTQ movement. To address these challenges, activists must cultivate spaces that encourage vulnerability, honesty, and mutual respect.

Practical Examples

Alec Butler has championed various initiatives aimed at bridging cultural divides within the LGBTQ movement. One notable example is the *Cultural Exchange Program*, which pairs LGBTQ individuals from different backgrounds to share their stories, experiences, and cultural practices. This initiative not only fosters understanding but also celebrates the rich diversity within the LGBTQ community.

Another example is the annual *Unity Festival*, organized by a coalition of LGBTQ organizations representing various cultural backgrounds. The festival features workshops, performances, and discussions that highlight the intersectionality of identities. By creating a platform for dialogue, the Unity Festival encourages participants to engage with issues that affect different communities, promoting solidarity and collaboration.

Creating Safe Spaces for Dialogue

To effectively encourage dialogue, it is essential to create safe spaces where individuals feel comfortable sharing their experiences. This involves establishing ground rules for discussions that prioritize respect, active listening, and openness to different perspectives. Facilitators can play a crucial role in guiding conversations, ensuring that all voices are heard, and addressing any tensions that arise.

Furthermore, integrating cultural competency training into LGBTQ organizations can equip activists with the tools necessary to navigate complex cultural dynamics. Understanding the cultural contexts of different communities allows for more meaningful engagement and reduces the likelihood of misunderstandings.

Conclusion

In conclusion, encouraging dialogue and understanding between different cultural communities is vital for the advancement of the LGBTQ movement. By embracing intersectionality, addressing challenges, and implementing practical strategies, activists like Alec Butler can foster a more inclusive and united movement. Through dialogue, we can dismantle barriers, celebrate diversity, and create a future where all identities are honored and respected. As we continue to advocate for equality, let us remember that our strength lies in our ability to listen, learn, and grow together.

Fostering unity among marginalized groups

The journey toward equality and acceptance for marginalized communities is not a solitary path; it is a collective endeavor that thrives on unity and collaboration. In the context of Alec Butler's activism, fostering unity among marginalized groups is not merely an ideal but a necessary strategy for amplifying voices and creating meaningful change. This section explores the theoretical foundations, challenges, and practical examples of fostering such unity, emphasizing its critical importance in the broader LGBTQ movement.

Theoretical Foundations

At the heart of fostering unity among marginalized groups lies the concept of intersectionality, a term coined by Kimberlé Crenshaw in 1989. Intersectionality posits that individuals experience oppression and privilege in varying degrees based on multiple social identities, including race, gender, sexuality, and class. This framework encourages activists to recognize and address the interconnectedness of various forms of discrimination, fostering a more inclusive approach to advocacy.

The equation representing intersectionality can be expressed as:

$$O = f(I_1, I_2, I_3, \ldots, I_n) \tag{12}$$

where O represents the overall oppression experienced by an individual, and I_n represents the various intersecting identities (e.g., race, gender, sexuality). This equation illustrates that oppression cannot be understood through a singular lens; rather, it is a complex interplay of multiple identities.

Challenges to Unity

Despite the theoretical underpinnings that advocate for unity, several challenges persist in fostering collaboration among marginalized groups. These challenges include:

+ **Historical Divisions:** Many marginalized groups have historically been pitted against one another due to competition for resources, recognition, and representation. This can lead to distrust and reluctance to collaborate, as seen in the tensions between various factions within the LGBTQ community and other marginalized groups.

+ **Differing Priorities:** Each marginalized group often has specific issues that are paramount to their community. For example, while LGBTQ activists may prioritize issues such as marriage equality and anti-discrimination laws, Indigenous activists may focus on land rights and cultural preservation. These differing priorities can create barriers to collaboration.

+ **Tokenism and Representation:** There is a risk of tokenism when marginalized groups are included in discussions or initiatives without genuine commitment to their needs and perspectives. This can result in superficial unity that fails to address the deeper issues at play.

Practical Examples of Fostering Unity

Alec Butler's advocacy work exemplifies the importance of fostering unity among marginalized groups. Through various initiatives, Butler has actively sought to bridge gaps between different communities. Here are some notable examples:

+ **Collaborative Activism:** Butler has organized events that bring together LGBTQ activists and Indigenous leaders to discuss shared struggles and strategies for advocacy. These events create safe spaces for dialogue, allowing participants to share their experiences and learn from one another.

+ **Intersectional Campaigns:** In campaigns addressing issues such as homelessness or mental health, Butler emphasizes the importance of recognizing how intersecting identities impact individuals' experiences. By highlighting stories from diverse voices, these campaigns foster solidarity and understanding among various marginalized groups.

◆ **Mentorship Programs:** Butler has initiated mentorship programs that connect young LGBTQ individuals with mentors from other marginalized communities. This initiative not only empowers youth but also encourages cross-community relationships that can lead to collaborative efforts in advocacy.

Conclusion

Fostering unity among marginalized groups is essential for creating a more equitable society. By embracing intersectionality, acknowledging challenges, and actively engaging in collaborative efforts, activists like Alec Butler can pave the way for a future where all voices are heard and valued. As the LGBTQ movement continues to evolve, the importance of solidarity and unity will remain a cornerstone of effective advocacy, ensuring that the fight for equality is not just for one group but for all marginalized identities.

In conclusion, the journey toward unity is ongoing, requiring continuous effort, empathy, and understanding. It is through this collective approach that true change can be achieved, fostering a society that celebrates diversity and champions the rights of all individuals, regardless of their identity.

Creating safe spaces for all identities

In the ever-evolving landscape of LGBTQ activism, the creation of safe spaces for all identities emerges as a crucial pillar for fostering inclusivity, understanding, and solidarity. Safe spaces are environments where individuals can express their identities without fear of discrimination, judgment, or violence. They are essential for marginalized groups, particularly within the LGBTQ community, as they provide a sanctuary for self-exploration and affirmation.

The concept of safe spaces is deeply rooted in the theory of intersectionality, which posits that individuals experience multiple, overlapping identities that can create unique challenges and forms of discrimination. Coined by legal scholar Kimberlé Crenshaw, intersectionality highlights how race, gender, sexuality, and other social identities intersect to shape individual experiences. This framework is essential when discussing the creation of safe spaces, as it underscores the need for environments that consider the diverse identities within the LGBTQ community.

The Importance of Safe Spaces

Creating safe spaces is not merely about physical locations; it involves fostering an ethos of acceptance and understanding. These spaces allow individuals to share their experiences, foster connections, and engage in dialogue that challenges societal norms. For example, community centers, LGBTQ youth groups, and online forums can serve as safe havens where individuals can explore their identities without fear of backlash.

However, the creation of safe spaces also presents challenges. One of the primary issues is the risk of exclusion within these spaces. While the intention is to create an inclusive environment, it is crucial to ensure that the needs of all marginalized identities are addressed. For instance, a space that primarily focuses on gay male experiences may inadvertently alienate transgender or non-binary individuals. To combat this, it is essential to actively seek input from diverse community members and incorporate their perspectives into the design and operation of safe spaces.

Examples of Successful Safe Spaces

Several organizations and initiatives have successfully created safe spaces that prioritize intersectionality and inclusivity. One notable example is the *Two-Spirit* community, which emphasizes the importance of recognizing and celebrating Indigenous identities alongside LGBTQ identities. Programs such as the *Two-Spirit Gathering* provide a platform for Indigenous LGBTQ individuals to come together, share their experiences, and foster a sense of community. These gatherings not only create safe spaces but also empower participants to reclaim their cultural heritage and identity.

Another example is the establishment of *LGBTQ+ youth centers*, which offer resources, support, and a safe environment for young people navigating their identities. These centers often provide counseling, educational workshops, and social activities that promote inclusivity. By focusing on the unique challenges faced by LGBTQ youth, these centers create an environment where individuals can thrive and develop a positive sense of self.

Challenges in Maintaining Safe Spaces

Despite the importance of safe spaces, maintaining them can be fraught with difficulties. One significant challenge is the external societal pressures that can infiltrate these environments. For instance, instances of hate crimes or discrimination can create a sense of fear and vulnerability, undermining the very purpose of safe spaces. To combat this, it is vital for safe spaces to have clear policies and protocols in place to address incidents of discrimination and to support individuals who may experience trauma.

Additionally, the evolution of language and identity within the LGBTQ community necessitates ongoing education and training for those who facilitate safe spaces. Language is a powerful tool in shaping perceptions and experiences; thus, it is essential to create an environment where individuals feel comfortable discussing their identities and the terminology that best represents them. Regular workshops and discussions can help foster a culture of learning and adaptability, ensuring that safe spaces remain relevant and responsive to the needs of their communities.

Conclusion

In conclusion, creating safe spaces for all identities is a fundamental aspect of LGBTQ activism that requires intentionality, inclusivity, and ongoing dialogue. By grounding these spaces in the principles of intersectionality, activists can ensure that they address the diverse needs of marginalized communities. Through the establishment of supportive environments, individuals can find solace, empowerment, and a sense of belonging. Ultimately, safe spaces not only contribute to individual well-being but also strengthen the collective fight for equality and justice within the broader LGBTQ movement.

Making waves in the media

Becoming a media personality

Guest appearances on talk shows and news programs

Alec Butler's foray into the media landscape began as a natural extension of their activism. Recognizing the power of visibility, Alec embraced opportunities to appear on talk shows and news programs, understanding that these platforms could amplify their message and reach a broader audience.

The Power of Media Representation

Media representation plays a crucial role in shaping societal perceptions of marginalized communities. According to Hall's (1997) theory of representation, the way individuals and groups are portrayed in the media significantly influences public understanding and attitudes. For Alec, appearing on popular talk shows provided a chance to challenge stereotypes and present a nuanced view of the LGBTQ experience, particularly from the perspective of a Two-Spirit individual.

Strategic Appearances

Alec's strategy involved selecting programs that aligned with their values and reached diverse audiences. For instance, their appearance on a nationally televised talk show not only showcased their artistic talents but also allowed them to discuss pressing LGBTQ issues, such as the need for inclusive policies and the importance of mental health support for LGBTQ youth.

Engaging with the Audience

During these appearances, Alec utilized a blend of personal storytelling and factual information to engage viewers. By sharing their own journey of self-discovery and activism, they created an emotional connection with the audience, fostering empathy and understanding. For example, during a segment on a popular morning show, Alec recounted their experiences growing up in a rural community, facing discrimination, and ultimately finding empowerment through activism. This approach resonated with many viewers, prompting discussions around acceptance and the importance of community support.

Addressing Controversial Topics

Alec did not shy away from addressing controversial topics during their media appearances. They tackled issues such as the ongoing violence against LGBTQ individuals, particularly focusing on the intersectionality of race and gender within the community. By highlighting the struggles faced by Two-Spirit individuals, Alec brought attention to the unique challenges that often go unnoticed in mainstream discussions.

For instance, during a panel discussion on a news program, Alec stated:

> "Two-Spirit people have historically been the bridge between genders in Indigenous cultures. Yet today, many face discrimination not only from society at large but also within their own communities. It's essential to amplify these voices and advocate for their rights."

This powerful statement emphasized the need for intersectional advocacy and sparked meaningful dialogue among panelists and viewers alike.

Navigating Backlash

While Alec's appearances garnered significant support, they also faced backlash from conservative audiences and detractors. Critics often attempted to undermine their message, labeling it as divisive or radical. However, Alec viewed this backlash as an opportunity for education. They responded to criticism with grace, using it as a platform to further articulate their beliefs and advocate for understanding.

For example, after a particularly contentious interview, Alec took to social media to address the backlash, stating:

> "I welcome dialogue, even when it's uncomfortable. It's through these conversations that we can begin to bridge gaps and foster understanding. Let's keep the conversation going."

This response not only showcased Alec's resilience but also reinforced their commitment to advocacy and education.

Impact on Public Discourse

Alec's media appearances have had a lasting impact on public discourse surrounding LGBTQ issues in Canada. By bringing visibility to the Two-Spirit experience and advocating for inclusive policies, they have contributed to a broader cultural shift towards acceptance and understanding. Their presence on talk shows and news programs has encouraged other LGBTQ individuals to share their stories, fostering a sense of community and solidarity.

In conclusion, Alec Butler's guest appearances on talk shows and news programs have been instrumental in shaping public perceptions of LGBTQ issues. By leveraging the power of media representation, they have not only amplified their voice but also inspired countless others to embrace their identities and advocate for equality. The impact of these appearances extends far beyond the screen, igniting conversations and encouraging a more inclusive society.

Providing commentary on LGBTQ issues in the media

Alec Butler's emergence as a media personality marked a significant turning point in the dialogue surrounding LGBTQ issues in Canada. By leveraging various platforms, Alec not only provided commentary but also challenged prevailing narratives that often marginalized LGBTQ voices. This section explores how Alec utilized media as a tool for advocacy and the impact of this engagement on public perception and policy.

The Role of Media in Shaping LGBTQ Discourse

Media serves as a powerful conduit for shaping societal attitudes and beliefs. According to the *Framing Theory*, the way issues are presented in the media can significantly influence public perception. For LGBTQ issues, this framing often oscillates between visibility and invisibility, acceptance and rejection. Alec Butler's commentary sought to disrupt negative stereotypes and promote a more nuanced understanding of LGBTQ identities.

Engaging in Public Discourse

Alec's appearances on talk shows and news programs provided a platform to articulate the complexities of LGBTQ experiences. For instance, during a widely viewed national broadcast, Alec addressed the intersectionality of race, gender, and sexuality, highlighting the unique challenges faced by Two-Spirit individuals. This commentary not only educated the audience but also humanized the struggles of marginalized communities.

$$\text{Visibility} = \frac{\text{Representation}}{\text{Misrepresentation}} \tag{13}$$

This equation illustrates the delicate balance between visibility and misrepresentation in media portrayals. Alec's efforts to increase positive representation contributed to a growing acceptance of LGBTQ individuals in Canadian society. By sharing personal narratives and advocating for inclusive policies, Alec became a voice for those often silenced.

Addressing Key Issues

In providing commentary, Alec focused on several critical issues affecting the LGBTQ community:

+ **Mental Health:** Alec highlighted the mental health crisis within the LGBTQ community, particularly among youth. By discussing the impact of discrimination and social isolation, Alec called for increased mental health resources tailored to LGBTQ individuals.

+ **Legal Rights:** Through public commentary, Alec underscored the ongoing legal battles for equal rights, including marriage equality and anti-discrimination protections. This advocacy was pivotal in influencing public opinion and legislative action.

+ **Cultural Representation:** Alec championed the importance of authentic representation in media and the arts. By critiquing stereotypical portrayals of LGBTQ characters in film and television, Alec encouraged creators to tell more diverse and accurate stories.

Impact of Social Media Engagement

With the rise of social media, Alec expanded their reach beyond traditional media outlets. Platforms like Twitter and Instagram became vital for disseminating information and mobilizing support. Alec utilized these platforms to engage in real-time discussions about current events affecting the LGBTQ community, such as the backlash against trans rights legislation.

$$\text{Engagement} = \text{Followers} \times \text{Content Quality} \tag{14}$$

This equation emphasizes the relationship between an activist's following and the quality of their content in driving engagement. Alec's ability to create compelling, informative posts led to a significant increase in followers and engagement rates, amplifying their message.

Challenges and Backlash

Despite the positive impact of Alec's commentary, they faced significant challenges, including backlash from conservative groups and individuals resistant to change. Instances of online harassment and misrepresentation in the media tested Alec's resolve. However, these challenges also provided opportunities for education and dialogue. Alec often addressed criticism head-on, using it as a chance to clarify misconceptions and advocate for understanding.

Conclusion

Alec Butler's contributions to media commentary on LGBTQ issues exemplify the power of unfiltered voices in shaping public discourse. By addressing critical issues, engaging with diverse audiences, and navigating the complexities of media representation, Alec not only raised awareness but also inspired a generation of activists to embrace their identities and advocate for equality. Their work serves as a reminder of the importance of visibility and representation in the ongoing struggle for LGBTQ rights.

Writing articles and opinion pieces for renowned publications

Alec Butler's foray into writing articles and opinion pieces for renowned publications marked a significant evolution in their activism. This chapter of their journey not only amplified their voice but also solidified their position as a thought leader within the LGBTQ community and beyond. Writing became a powerful tool for advocacy, allowing Alec to articulate pressing issues, share personal narratives, and mobilize support for the LGBTQ cause.

The Power of Written Expression

Writing serves as a potent form of expression, particularly in the realm of activism. According to [?], the written word has the ability to educate, empower, and inspire action. For Alec, this meant using their platform to address systemic inequalities faced by LGBTQ individuals, especially those who identify as Two-Spirit. Through articles and opinion pieces, Alec could dissect complex issues, such as discrimination in healthcare, violence against LGBTQ individuals, and the intersectionality of race and gender within the community.

Identifying Key Issues

In crafting their articles, Alec identified key issues that resonated with both the LGBTQ community and the general public. For instance, one notable piece titled "Two-Spirit Voices: Bridging Cultures and Communities" highlighted the unique struggles faced by Two-Spirit individuals within Indigenous and LGBTQ spaces. This article not only educated readers about the Two-Spirit identity but also called for greater representation and understanding within both communities.

Engaging with Renowned Publications

Alec strategically targeted renowned publications known for their progressive stances on social issues. By contributing to platforms such as *The Globe and Mail*, *HuffPost*, and *The Advocate*, Alec was able to reach a wider audience and engage in meaningful discourse. The selection of these platforms was not arbitrary; each publication has a history of advocating for marginalized voices, making them ideal venues for Alec's message.

The Art of Persuasion

The effectiveness of Alec's writing can be attributed to their mastery of persuasive techniques. Drawing on the principles of rhetoric, as outlined by [?], Alec employed ethos, pathos, and logos to craft compelling narratives. By establishing credibility (ethos), appealing to the emotions of readers (pathos), and presenting logical arguments (logos), Alec was able to sway public opinion and foster empathy for the LGBTQ community.

$$\text{Persuasion} = \text{Ethos} + \text{Pathos} + \text{Logos} \qquad (15)$$

This equation encapsulates the balance necessary for effective advocacy through writing. Each component plays a crucial role in ensuring that the message resonates with the audience, thereby maximizing impact.

Addressing Controversial Topics

Alec did not shy away from addressing controversial topics in their writing. For instance, an opinion piece titled "The Reality of Transphobia in Canada" sparked significant discussion and debate. In this article, Alec shared personal experiences and statistical data to highlight the prevalence of transphobia, urging readers to confront their biases and engage in allyship. The piece was met with both support and backlash, illustrating the contentious nature of LGBTQ discourse in society.

Utilizing Social Media as a Catalyst

In addition to traditional publications, Alec leveraged social media to amplify their written work. By sharing links to their articles on platforms such as Twitter and Instagram, Alec could reach diverse audiences and encourage dialogue. The interactivity of social media also allowed readers to engage directly with Alec, fostering a sense of community and shared purpose.

Measuring Impact

The impact of Alec's writings is evident in the discussions they ignited and the awareness they raised. Metrics such as readership statistics, social media engagement, and subsequent conversations in the media can be indicative of their influence. For example, after publishing an article on the need for inclusive policies in schools, Alec noted a surge in discussions surrounding LGBTQ inclusivity in educational settings, with several institutions reaching out to implement changes.

Conclusion

In conclusion, Alec Butler's contributions to renowned publications exemplify the power of the written word in activism. Through strategic engagement with key issues, mastery of persuasive techniques, and effective use of social media, Alec has not only amplified their voice but has also inspired others to join the fight for equality. Their writings serve as a testament to the importance of unfiltered voices in the LGBTQ movement, paving the way for future generations of activists to share their stories and advocate for change.

Utilizing social media to reach a wider audience

In the digital age, social media has emerged as a powerful tool for activists, enabling them to amplify their voices and connect with a global audience. For Alec Butler, harnessing the potential of platforms such as Twitter, Instagram, and Facebook was not just a strategic move; it was a revolutionary approach to advocacy.

Theoretical Framework

The utilization of social media in activism can be understood through the lens of *network theory*, which posits that individuals and organizations are interconnected through various social ties. According to Granovetter's (1973) concept of *weak ties*, relationships that are less intimate can often be more effective in spreading information across diverse networks. This theory underlines the importance of social media in activism, as it allows for the dissemination of messages beyond immediate social circles, reaching individuals who may not be directly involved in the LGBTQ community.

Challenges and Limitations

Despite its potential, social media activism is not without its challenges. One significant issue is the phenomenon of *slacktivism*, where individuals engage in minimal effort actions, such as liking or sharing posts, without committing to more substantial forms of activism. This raises questions about the effectiveness of social media campaigns. Furthermore, the digital divide remains a critical barrier; not all marginalized communities have equal access to technology or the internet, potentially excluding them from conversations and movements that are crucial for their representation.

Alec Butler's Strategy

Alec Butler recognized the dual-edged nature of social media and approached it with a strategic mindset. By crafting compelling narratives and engaging visuals, Alec was able to capture the attention of a broad audience. For instance, through Instagram, Alec shared personal stories of their journey as a Two-Spirit individual, intertwining artistic expression with activism. This not only humanized the issues at hand but also fostered a sense of community among followers.

$$\text{Engagement Rate} = \frac{\text{Total Engagements}}{\text{Total Followers}} \times 100 \qquad (16)$$

By monitoring engagement rates, Alec was able to refine their content strategy, focusing on posts that resonated with their audience. This data-driven approach ensured that their message was not only heard but also acted upon.

Case Studies

One notable example of Alec's effective use of social media was during the 2019 Pride Month. Through a series of posts, Alec highlighted the intersectionality of

LGBTQ issues with Indigenous rights, using hashtags like #TwoSpiritPride and #IndigenousVoices. This campaign not only garnered significant attention but also sparked conversations across various platforms, leading to increased visibility for Two-Spirit issues within the broader LGBTQ discourse.

Another instance was Alec's response to a wave of anti-LGBTQ legislation in Canada. Utilizing Twitter, Alec organized a virtual rally, encouraging followers to share their stories and experiences using the hashtag #StandWithUs. This initiative not only mobilized supporters but also attracted media coverage, amplifying the reach of the message.

Conclusion

In conclusion, Alec Butler's adept use of social media exemplifies the transformative power of digital platforms in modern activism. By strategically navigating the complexities of online engagement, Alec was able to connect with a wider audience, raise awareness, and foster community. However, it is essential to remain cognizant of the limitations and challenges inherent in social media activism, ensuring that efforts translate into meaningful change both online and offline. The journey of utilizing social media is ongoing, and as Alec continues to evolve, so too does the landscape of LGBTQ advocacy in the digital realm.

Facing backlash and criticism

Confronting homophobic and transphobic attacks

In the journey of activism, confronting homophobic and transphobic attacks is an essential aspect of advocating for LGBTQ rights. These attacks can manifest in various forms, including verbal harassment, physical violence, systemic discrimination, and media misrepresentation. Alec Butler, as a prominent Two-Spirit LGBTQ activist, faced numerous challenges throughout their career, but their resilience and commitment to advocacy turned these adversities into opportunities for education and change.

Homophobia and transphobia are rooted in societal norms that perpetuate binary understandings of gender and sexuality. Theories such as Judith Butler's concept of gender performativity suggest that gender is not an inherent quality but rather a set of behaviors and performances that society imposes. This theory underscores the importance of challenging traditional notions of gender and sexuality, which often lead to discrimination and violence against those who do not conform.

One significant example of the impact of these attacks on Alec's life occurred during a public speaking engagement. While discussing the importance of Two-Spirit representation in the LGBTQ community, Alec encountered a hostile audience member who shouted derogatory remarks. Instead of allowing this to silence them, Alec turned the situation into a teachable moment. They addressed the individual directly, emphasizing the need for understanding and empathy. This confrontation not only highlighted the ongoing struggles faced by LGBTQ individuals but also showcased the power of standing firm against discrimination.

Moreover, the rise of social media has amplified both support and backlash for LGBTQ activists. Alec experienced a wave of transphobic comments after a viral video of their performance was shared online. In response, they utilized their platform to educate their followers about the harmful effects of transphobia and the importance of allyship. By engaging with their audience through thoughtful responses, Alec transformed a negative experience into a rallying cry for solidarity and support within the LGBTQ community.

The impact of homophobic and transphobic attacks extends beyond the individual level; it affects the broader community as well. Research has shown that such attacks can lead to increased levels of anxiety, depression, and other mental health issues among LGBTQ individuals. According to the *American Psychological Association*, experiences of discrimination can significantly affect one's psychological well-being, leading to a higher incidence of mental health disorders in marginalized populations.

To combat these issues, Alec engaged in grassroots activism, organizing workshops and community discussions aimed at raising awareness about the effects of homophobia and transphobia. They collaborated with mental health professionals to provide resources and support for those affected by discrimination. This approach not only addressed the immediate needs of individuals but also fostered a sense of community and resilience among LGBTQ individuals.

Furthermore, confronting these attacks requires a multifaceted approach that includes legal advocacy. Alec worked closely with LGBTQ organizations to push for policy changes that protect individuals from discrimination based on sexual orientation and gender identity. This advocacy is crucial, as legal protections can significantly reduce the incidence of hate crimes and discrimination. For instance, the implementation of hate crime legislation in Canada has been a vital step toward safeguarding the rights of LGBTQ individuals, although challenges remain in its enforcement.

In conclusion, confronting homophobic and transphobic attacks is a critical aspect of LGBTQ activism. Through personal resilience, community engagement, and legal advocacy, activists like Alec Butler have demonstrated that it is possible to turn adversity into empowerment. By addressing these issues head-on, they not only advocate for their own rights but also pave the way for future generations of LGBTQ activists to live authentically and without fear. The journey is ongoing, and the fight against homophobia and transphobia remains a vital component of the broader struggle for equality and acceptance.

Dealing with media misrepresentation and sensationalism

In the age of information, the media wields significant power over public perception, especially regarding marginalized communities. For Alec Butler, navigating this landscape has been fraught with challenges, particularly in dealing with media misrepresentation and sensationalism. This section explores the theoretical frameworks surrounding media representation, the specific problems faced by LGBTQ activists, and examples from Alec's experiences that illuminate these issues.

Theoretical Frameworks

Media representation theory posits that the way groups are portrayed in media can shape societal attitudes and beliefs about those groups. Stuart Hall's encoding/decoding model emphasizes the role of both media producers and audiences in the meaning-making process. According to Hall, media texts are encoded with particular messages by their creators, yet audiences decode these messages through their own cultural lenses. This can lead to a significant gap between the intended message and the audience's interpretation, especially when the media fails to accurately represent marginalized identities.

$$\text{Representation} = \text{Encoding} + \text{Decoding} \tag{17}$$

When it comes to LGBTQ representation, sensationalism often distorts the realities of individuals' lives, reducing complex identities to mere stereotypes or dramatic narratives. This is particularly true for Two-Spirit individuals, who often find their experiences oversimplified or sensationalized in mainstream media.

Problems Faced by LGBTQ Activists

Alec Butler has faced numerous instances of misrepresentation in the media, which can undermine the authenticity of their activism. One significant problem is the tendency of media outlets to focus on sensational aspects of LGBTQ lives, such as scandal, conflict, or tragedy, while neglecting the broader societal issues that affect these communities. This not only skews public perception but also diverts attention from critical discussions surrounding systemic discrimination and the need for policy change.

Additionally, the media often lacks a nuanced understanding of Two-Spirit identities, leading to mischaracterizations that can perpetuate harmful stereotypes. This lack of representation can further alienate Two-Spirit individuals from both the broader LGBTQ community and their Indigenous cultures.

Examples from Alec's Experience

Alec's journey has been marked by several instances of media misrepresentation. For example, during a public speaking engagement addressing the challenges faced by Two-Spirit individuals, a local news outlet sensationalized Alec's message, framing it as a dramatic confrontation rather than a call for understanding and solidarity. The headline read, "Two-Spirit Activist Shocks Audience with Bold Claims!" This framing not only misrepresented Alec's intent but also overshadowed the critical issues they were advocating for.

In another instance, a popular talk show invited Alec to discuss LGBTQ rights but focused predominantly on personal anecdotes rather than the structural inequalities faced by the community. The segment was edited to highlight emotional moments, reinforcing the stereotype of LGBTQ individuals as perpetual victims rather than empowered activists. This selective editing exemplifies how media can distort narratives to fit sensationalist agendas, ultimately undermining the voices of those it seeks to portray.

Turning Adversity into Opportunities

Despite these challenges, Alec has learned to navigate media interactions strategically. By preparing key messages and emphasizing the importance of accurate representation, they have turned potential misrepresentations into opportunities for education. Alec often uses interviews to clarify misconceptions, employing the platform to advocate for a more nuanced understanding of Two-Spirit identities and the broader LGBTQ movement.

Moreover, Alec has embraced social media as a tool to counteract misrepresentation. By sharing their experiences directly with followers, they can bypass traditional media channels that may distort their message. This approach empowers Alec to take control of their narrative, fostering a more authentic connection with their audience.

$$\text{Empowerment} = \text{Control of Narrative} + \text{Direct Engagement} \quad (18)$$

In conclusion, dealing with media misrepresentation and sensationalism is a significant challenge for LGBTQ activists like Alec Butler. By understanding the theoretical frameworks that underpin media representation, recognizing the problems posed by sensationalist narratives, and leveraging their experiences to educate and empower, Alec continues to advocate for a more accurate and respectful portrayal of LGBTQ identities in the media. This ongoing struggle highlights the critical importance of unfiltered voices in the fight for equality and representation.

Turning adversity into opportunities for education and change

In the tumultuous landscape of activism, adversity often emerges as a formidable challenge. However, for Alec Butler, each setback became a stepping stone towards greater awareness and transformation within the LGBTQ community. This section explores how Alec harnessed the power of adversity, converting it into a catalyst for education and change.

The Nature of Adversity

Adversity can take many forms, from personal attacks to systemic discrimination. In Alec's journey, encounters with homophobic and transphobic backlash were not merely obstacles; they were pivotal moments that shaped their activism. The theory of resilience, as posited by psychologists such as [?], suggests that individuals who face significant challenges can develop a heightened capacity to cope and thrive. Alec exemplified this resilience, using their experiences to fuel their advocacy.

Educational Outreach

One of the primary ways Alec transformed adversity into educational opportunities was through outreach programs. After facing public backlash, Alec recognized a gap in understanding within the broader community regarding LGBTQ issues. This realization led to the creation of workshops and seminars aimed at educating both LGBTQ individuals and their allies. These sessions often included discussions on the following key topics:

+ The significance of Two-Spirit identities in Indigenous cultures.

+ The impact of systemic discrimination on mental health within LGBTQ populations.

+ Strategies for allies to effectively support marginalized voices.

Alec's workshops not only provided crucial information but also fostered a sense of community and solidarity among participants. By sharing their own experiences, Alec encouraged attendees to engage in open dialogues about their struggles and triumphs, thereby normalizing conversations around difficult topics.

Media Engagement as a Tool for Change

Alec's encounters with media misrepresentation also served as a powerful impetus for change. Faced with sensationalized portrayals of their activism, Alec took to various platforms to set the record straight. They utilized social media as a tool for education, crafting posts that dissected misinformation and provided factual insights into LGBTQ issues. This approach aligns with the theory of critical media literacy, which emphasizes the importance of analyzing media messages to understand their societal implications [?].

For example, after a particularly egregious misrepresentation in a local news outlet, Alec responded with a well-articulated video that addressed the inaccuracies while educating viewers about the realities of LGBTQ life in Canada. This proactive stance not only countered the negative narrative but also empowered viewers to become advocates for accurate representation.

Community Engagement and Collaboration

Alec's strategy for turning adversity into opportunity also involved collaboration with other activists and organizations. By joining forces with groups focused on anti-bullying campaigns and mental health awareness, Alec expanded the reach of their message. This intersectional approach is supported by the concept of *collective efficacy*, which suggests that when individuals unite towards a common goal, their combined efforts can lead to significant change [?].

Through collaborative projects, such as community art installations and public awareness campaigns, Alec was able to address the stigma surrounding LGBTQ identities while also providing resources for those in need. For instance, a joint initiative with local schools aimed to create safe spaces for LGBTQ youth, fostering environments where students could express themselves without fear of discrimination.

Empowering Future Generations

Alec's commitment to education extended beyond immediate community outreach. Recognizing the importance of empowering future generations, they established scholarships and mentorship programs for LGBTQ youth interested in the arts and activism. By providing financial support and guidance, Alec aimed to cultivate a new wave of advocates who could carry the torch forward.

The impact of these initiatives is profound. Research shows that mentorship plays a crucial role in the development of young activists, providing them with the tools and confidence needed to navigate their own journeys [?]. Through their mentorship, Alec instilled a sense of purpose and resilience in young individuals, encouraging them to view adversity as an opportunity for growth rather than a barrier.

Conclusion

In conclusion, Alec Butler's ability to turn adversity into opportunities for education and change serves as a powerful testament to the resilience of the human spirit. By leveraging their experiences, Alec not only educated others but also fostered a sense of community, collaboration, and empowerment. This transformative approach not only addressed immediate challenges but also laid the groundwork for a more inclusive and understanding society. In the words of Alec, "Adversity is not the end; it's merely a beginning—a chance to rise, to educate, and to inspire."

The growth of Alec's platform and influence

As Alec Butler navigated the tumultuous waters of activism and artistry, their platform began to expand exponentially, fueled by a potent combination of authenticity, resilience, and a commitment to unfiltered expression. This growth is not merely a reflection of personal ambition but a manifestation of the collective struggle for LGBTQ rights, visibility, and acceptance within society.

Alec's rise can be understood through the lens of social movement theory, particularly the concepts of resource mobilization and framing processes. Resource mobilization theory posits that the success of social movements depends on the availability of resources—be it financial, human, or social capital. Alec's ability to leverage their artistic talents and personal narrative became a crucial resource in building a platform that resonated with diverse audiences.

$$\text{Influence} = f(\text{Authenticity, Engagement, Visibility}) \qquad (19)$$

Where: - Influence is the measure of Alec's impact on the LGBTQ community and beyond. - Authenticity refers to the genuine representation of their Two-Spirit identity and experiences. - Engagement encompasses interactions with followers, activists, and the broader community. - Visibility denotes the presence in media, public speaking, and cultural events.

Alec's journey reflects a strategic engagement with media platforms, utilizing both traditional and digital avenues to amplify their voice. Guest appearances on popular talk shows and news programs allowed Alec to reach audiences who might not be familiar with LGBTQ issues, effectively framing these discussions within the context of human rights and social justice. For instance, during a widely viewed interview on a national network, Alec articulated the importance of Two-Spirit representation, challenging viewers to reconsider their preconceived notions about gender and sexuality.

Furthermore, Alec's social media presence became a powerful tool for influence. By sharing personal stories, artistic creations, and activism updates, they fostered a sense of community among followers. The viral nature of social media meant that a single post could reach thousands, if not millions, creating a ripple effect that sparked conversations around LGBTQ rights. This is particularly evident in campaigns such as #TwoSpiritVisibility, which Alec spearheaded, encouraging individuals to share their own stories and experiences.

The growth of Alec's platform also brought challenges, including backlash and criticism from conservative factions. However, rather than stifling their voice, these adversities became opportunities for education and dialogue. Alec's response to such backlash often involved addressing misconceptions head-on, using the platform to educate detractors while simultaneously reinforcing their commitment to advocacy.

$$\text{Resilience} = \frac{\text{Response to Criticism}}{\text{Impact on Mental Health}} \quad (20)$$

Where: - Resilience indicates Alec's ability to withstand and grow from criticism. - Response to Criticism is the constructive engagement with detractors. - Impact on Mental Health reflects the psychological toll of public scrutiny.

An exemplary moment of this resilience occurred after Alec faced transphobic attacks during a public appearance. Instead of retreating, they organized a follow-up event titled "Voices Unfiltered," which focused on mental health and support for LGBTQ individuals facing similar challenges. This initiative not only solidified Alec's position as a leader in the community but also highlighted the importance of mental health resources for marginalized groups.

As Alec's platform expanded, so did their influence within policy-making circles. They began to engage with lawmakers and participate in discussions aimed at creating equitable policies for LGBTQ individuals. Alec's ability to articulate the lived experiences of Two-Spirit individuals and the broader LGBTQ community positioned them as a credible advocate for change. Their testimony during legislative hearings on anti-discrimination laws exemplified how personal narratives can influence policy decisions, illustrating the power of storytelling in activism.

$$\text{Policy Influence} = \text{Testimony} + \text{Public Support} \qquad (21)$$

Where: - Policy Influence is the effect Alec has on legislative changes. - Testimony includes personal stories shared in formal settings. - Public Support reflects the backing from community members and allies.

The culmination of these efforts has positioned Alec Butler not just as an activist but as a beacon of hope and change within the LGBTQ movement. Their platform continues to grow, inspiring others to embrace their identities and advocate for equality. The journey of Alec Butler serves as a testament to the impact of unfiltered voices in the fight for social justice, reminding us that influence is not merely about numbers but about the authenticity of one's message and the courage to speak out against injustice.

In conclusion, the growth of Alec's platform is a multifaceted phenomenon, intricately tied to their identity, experiences, and the broader socio-political landscape. As they continue to evolve as an artist and activist, Alec Butler's influence will undoubtedly leave a lasting mark on the LGBTQ movement, paving the way for future generations of advocates and changemakers.

Legacy and continuing the fight

Paving the way for future LGBTQ activists

Mentoring and supporting emerging LGBTQ voices

In the vibrant tapestry of activism, mentorship serves as a crucial thread, weaving together generations of advocates who dare to dream and demand change. Alec Butler, as a luminary in the LGBTQ movement, recognizes the profound impact of nurturing emerging voices. This section delves into the theoretical frameworks, challenges, and exemplary practices that underscore the importance of mentorship within the LGBTQ community.

Theoretical Frameworks

The concept of mentorship can be understood through various theoretical lenses. Social Learning Theory posits that individuals learn behaviors through observation and imitation of role models [?]. This is particularly relevant in the LGBTQ community, where young activists may lack visibility of successful figures who share their identities. Mentorship not only provides guidance but also fosters a sense of belonging and validation.

Furthermore, Intersectionality Theory, introduced by Kimberlé Crenshaw, emphasizes the interconnected nature of social categorizations such as race, gender, and sexual orientation [?]. Mentorship in the LGBTQ context must embrace this complexity, recognizing that emerging voices come from diverse backgrounds and experiences. Supporting these individuals requires an understanding of the unique challenges they face, including systemic discrimination and cultural barriers.

Challenges Faced by Emerging Voices

Despite the potential benefits of mentorship, emerging LGBTQ activists often encounter significant challenges. One primary obstacle is the scarcity of resources. Many LGBTQ youth come from marginalized backgrounds, facing economic hardships that limit their access to mentorship programs, workshops, and educational opportunities. According to a report by the Human Rights Campaign, LGBTQ youth are more likely to experience homelessness than their heterosexual peers, further exacerbating their vulnerabilities [?].

Additionally, the psychological toll of navigating a world rife with discrimination can hinder the confidence of emerging activists. The phenomenon of imposter syndrome, where individuals doubt their accomplishments and fear being exposed as a "fraud," is prevalent among LGBTQ youth [?]. This internal struggle can prevent them from seeking mentorship or fully engaging in activism.

Examples of Effective Mentorship Programs

Alec Butler's commitment to mentoring is exemplified through various initiatives aimed at uplifting emerging LGBTQ voices. One notable example is the "Two-Spirit Mentor Program," which pairs established Two-Spirit activists with younger individuals seeking guidance. This program not only fosters skill development but also emphasizes cultural heritage and identity, reinforcing the importance of Two-Spirit representation within the broader LGBTQ movement.

Another successful initiative is the "LGBTQ Youth Leadership Summit," an annual event that brings together young activists from across Canada. Participants engage in workshops, panels, and networking opportunities designed to empower them as future leaders. By providing a platform for young voices, this summit cultivates a sense of community and shared purpose, essential for sustained activism.

The Role of Storytelling in Mentorship

Storytelling emerges as a powerful tool in mentorship, allowing experienced activists to share their journeys, struggles, and triumphs. Alec Butler often utilizes storytelling to create a relatable narrative that resonates with emerging voices. By sharing personal experiences, mentors can demystify the path of activism and inspire confidence in their mentees.

Research indicates that storytelling enhances emotional connection and retention of information [?]. When mentors share their stories, they not only impart knowledge but also foster resilience in their mentees. This emotional bond is particularly vital in the LGBTQ community, where many young individuals may feel isolated or misunderstood.

Conclusion

In conclusion, mentoring and supporting emerging LGBTQ voices is not merely a responsibility; it is a transformative practice that shapes the future of activism. By leveraging theoretical frameworks, addressing challenges, and implementing effective programs, mentors like Alec Butler can empower the next generation to embrace their identities and advocate for change. As the LGBTQ movement continues to evolve, the importance of unfiltered voices remains paramount, ensuring that every story contributes to the collective narrative of resilience and hope.

Creating resources and platforms for LGBTQ youth

In the quest for equality and representation, Alec Butler recognized the urgent need for dedicated resources and platforms for LGBTQ youth. These young individuals often face unique challenges, including isolation, discrimination, and a lack of support systems. By creating spaces that empower, educate, and inspire, Alec aimed to pave the way for a more inclusive future.

Identifying the Challenges

LGBTQ youth often grapple with a myriad of issues that can hinder their personal development and mental health. According to the *Trevor Project*, LGBTQ youth are more than twice as likely to experience bullying compared to their heterosexual peers. This bullying often leads to higher rates of depression, anxiety, and suicidal ideation. Furthermore, many LGBTQ youth lack access to affirming resources, such as counseling and community support.

$$\text{Mental Health Risk} = \frac{\text{LGBTQ Youth}}{\text{Support Systems}} \tag{22}$$

This equation illustrates the inverse relationship between the mental health risks faced by LGBTQ youth and the availability of support systems. As the availability of supportive resources decreases, the mental health risks for these individuals increase.

Creating Safe Spaces

To combat these challenges, Alec Butler spearheaded initiatives aimed at creating safe spaces for LGBTQ youth. These spaces serve as havens where young people can express themselves freely, share their experiences, and connect with others who understand their struggles. For example, Alec collaborated with local community centers to establish weekly support groups that focus on issues relevant to LGBTQ youth, such as coming out, identity exploration, and dealing with societal pressures.

Educational Resources and Workshops

In addition to safe spaces, Alec recognized the importance of educational resources. Workshops and seminars were designed to provide LGBTQ youth with vital information about their rights, health, and well-being. Topics covered included:

- Understanding sexual orientation and gender identity

- Navigating the healthcare system

- Legal rights and protections for LGBTQ individuals

- Coping strategies for dealing with discrimination

These workshops not only empower youth with knowledge but also foster a sense of community and belonging. By equipping young people with the tools they need to advocate for themselves, Alec aimed to instill confidence and resilience.

Utilizing Technology and Social Media

In the digital age, technology plays a critical role in connecting LGBTQ youth with resources. Alec leveraged social media platforms to create online communities where young people could engage with one another, share their stories, and access valuable information. Initiatives such as the *Two-Spirit Youth Network* were launched, providing a digital space for Two-Spirit and LGBTQ youth to connect, share resources, and support one another.

$$\text{Community Engagement} = \text{Social Media} + \text{Resource Sharing} \quad (23)$$

This equation reflects the synergy between community engagement and the use of social media for resource sharing, highlighting the importance of digital platforms in fostering connections among LGBTQ youth.

Mentorship Programs

Recognizing the power of mentorship, Alec established programs that paired LGBTQ youth with mentors who had navigated similar experiences. These mentors provided guidance, support, and encouragement, helping young individuals to envision a future filled with possibilities. This one-on-one connection can be transformative, as it allows youth to see that their identities can be celebrated and embraced.

Advocacy and Policy Change

Alec's efforts extended beyond direct support for LGBTQ youth. They actively advocated for policy changes at the local and national levels, aiming to increase funding for LGBTQ programs in schools and community centers. By engaging with policymakers, Alec sought to ensure that LGBTQ youth have access to the resources they need to thrive.

Conclusion

Creating resources and platforms for LGBTQ youth is not just an act of advocacy; it is a vital investment in the future of the LGBTQ community. By empowering young individuals with knowledge, support, and a sense of belonging, Alec Butler has laid the groundwork for a more inclusive society. The legacy of these efforts continues to inspire future generations, reminding us all of the importance of nurturing the voices of our youth.

Establishing scholarships and grants for LGBTQ artists

In the quest to uplift and empower LGBTQ artists, establishing scholarships and grants has emerged as a vital strategy. These financial resources serve as both a recognition of talent and a means to mitigate the systemic barriers that LGBTQ individuals often face in pursuing careers in the arts.

The Importance of Financial Support

Financial constraints can significantly hinder the artistic ambitions of LGBTQ individuals. Many face economic hardships due to discrimination in the workplace, lack of familial support, or the high costs associated with artistic education and practice. According to a study by the National Endowment for the Arts, artists from marginalized communities are less likely to receive funding compared to their peers, which exacerbates existing inequalities in the arts. Thus, scholarships and grants specifically tailored for LGBTQ artists can provide crucial support, allowing them to focus on their craft without the burden of financial stress.

Types of Scholarships and Grants

There are various forms of scholarships and grants that can be established to support LGBTQ artists:

- **Merit-Based Scholarships:** These scholarships are awarded based on artistic talent and potential, encouraging LGBTQ artists to develop their skills and pursue their passions.

- **Need-Based Grants:** These grants focus on the financial need of the artist, ensuring that those who may not have the means to support their artistic endeavors can still access opportunities.

- **Project Grants:** These grants provide funding for specific artistic projects, allowing LGBTQ artists to bring their creative visions to life while addressing relevant social issues.

- **Fellowships:** Fellowships can offer a combination of financial support, mentorship, and networking opportunities, fostering the professional development of LGBTQ artists.

Examples of Existing Programs

Several organizations have already taken steps to establish scholarships and grants for LGBTQ artists. For instance:

- The **Queer Artists Fund** provides grants to LGBTQ artists of all disciplines, enabling them to create new work and expand their artistic practice.

- The **Point Foundation** offers scholarships to LGBTQ students pursuing higher education, with a focus on those who demonstrate leadership and commitment to community service.

- The **Lambda Literary Foundation** runs the *Lambda Literary Awards* and provides fellowships to emerging LGBTQ writers, supporting their development and visibility in the literary world.

These programs not only provide financial assistance but also foster a sense of community and belonging among LGBTQ artists, which is essential for their personal and professional growth.

Challenges in Establishing Funding

Despite the importance of scholarships and grants, several challenges persist in establishing these funding opportunities:

- **Funding Sources:** Securing sustainable funding can be a significant barrier. Many LGBTQ organizations operate on limited budgets, making it difficult to allocate resources for scholarships and grants.

- **Awareness and Outreach:** Many potential applicants may not be aware of available scholarships and grants, particularly those in rural or underserved areas. Effective outreach strategies are essential to ensure that these opportunities reach those who need them most.

- **Evaluation Criteria:** Establishing fair and inclusive evaluation criteria for awarding scholarships and grants can be complex. It is crucial to ensure that the process is transparent and equitable, allowing diverse voices and experiences to be recognized.

Theoretical Frameworks for Support

The establishment of scholarships and grants for LGBTQ artists can be grounded in several theoretical frameworks, including:

- **Social Justice Theory:** This framework emphasizes the need for equity and access to resources, advocating for marginalized groups to receive the support necessary to thrive.

- **Intersectionality:** Recognizing the multiple identities that individuals hold, intersectionality highlights the importance of tailoring support to meet the unique challenges faced by LGBTQ artists from diverse backgrounds.

- **Cultural Capital:** Bourdieu's concept of cultural capital suggests that access to education and resources can enhance an individual's ability to succeed in the arts. Scholarships and grants serve as a means to increase cultural capital for LGBTQ artists.

Conclusion

Establishing scholarships and grants for LGBTQ artists is not merely a financial endeavor; it is a commitment to fostering diversity, inclusion, and representation in the arts. By investing in the talents and voices of LGBTQ individuals, we can create a richer, more vibrant cultural landscape that reflects the full spectrum of human experience. The legacy of such initiatives will not only support individual artists but also inspire future generations to embrace their identities and express themselves through art.

$$\text{Funding Success} = \text{Awareness} \times \text{Sustainability} \times \text{Inclusivity} \qquad (24)$$

Inspiring the next generation of activists through storytelling

Storytelling has long been recognized as a powerful tool for education, connection, and empowerment. In the realm of activism, particularly within the LGBTQ community, storytelling serves not only as a means of sharing personal experiences but also as a catalyst for inspiring others to engage in the fight for equality and justice. Alec Butler's commitment to storytelling as a form of activism highlights the vital role narratives play in shaping identities, fostering empathy, and galvanizing collective action.

Theoretical Framework

The significance of storytelling in activism can be understood through several theoretical lenses, including narrative theory, social identity theory, and the concept of counter-narratives. Narrative theory posits that stories are fundamental to human experience, allowing individuals to make sense of their lives and the world around them. According to Bruner (1991), narratives are not just a way to convey information; they shape our understanding of reality and our place within it. This is particularly pertinent for marginalized communities, where dominant narratives often exclude or misrepresent their experiences.

Social identity theory, developed by Tajfel and Turner (1979), suggests that individuals derive a sense of self from their group memberships. For LGBTQ individuals, storytelling can help affirm their identities and foster a sense of belonging within the community. By sharing their stories, activists like Alec Butler contribute to the creation of a collective identity that empowers others to embrace their own narratives.

Counter-narratives are essential in challenging dominant societal narratives that perpetuate discrimination and stigma. As articulated by Delgado and

Stefancic (2001), counter-narratives provide a means for marginalized voices to assert their experiences and perspectives, thereby contesting the dominant discourse. Alec's storytelling embodies this concept, as it confronts stereotypes and misconceptions about LGBTQ individuals, particularly those within Indigenous communities.

Challenges in Storytelling

While storytelling is a powerful tool for activism, it is not without its challenges. One significant issue is the risk of oversimplification or commodification of complex identities and experiences. As activists share their stories, there is a danger that their narratives may be reduced to mere slogans or sound bites, stripping them of their nuanced meanings. This can lead to the perpetuation of stereotypes rather than their dismantling.

Additionally, the act of sharing personal stories can be emotionally taxing for activists. Many individuals recount traumatic experiences of discrimination, violence, and rejection, which can take a toll on their mental health. It is crucial for activists to prioritize self-care and seek support when engaging in storytelling, ensuring that their advocacy does not come at the expense of their well-being.

Another challenge lies in the audience's reception of these stories. Not all listeners are open to understanding or empathizing with LGBTQ experiences. Activists must navigate the complexities of audience engagement, tailoring their narratives to resonate with diverse groups while remaining authentic to their lived experiences.

Examples of Storytelling in Activism

Alec Butler's own journey exemplifies the power of storytelling in inspiring future activists. Through a variety of mediums, including performances, public speaking, and written works, Alec has shared personal narratives that highlight the struggles and triumphs of being Two-Spirit and LGBTQ in Canada. For instance, in their acclaimed performance piece, "Voices of the Unheard," Alec weaves together stories from their life and the lives of other LGBTQ individuals, creating a tapestry of resilience and hope. This work not only entertains but also educates audiences about the unique challenges faced by Two-Spirit people, encouraging greater understanding and support.

Moreover, initiatives such as the "StoryCorps" project have demonstrated the impact of storytelling on community building and activism. By recording and sharing personal narratives, StoryCorps fosters connections among individuals from different backgrounds, promoting empathy and solidarity. This model can be particularly effective within the LGBTQ community, where shared experiences can create a sense of belonging and motivate collective action.

Another notable example is the "It Gets Better" campaign, which harnesses the power of personal storytelling to provide hope and encouragement to LGBTQ youth facing bullying and discrimination. By sharing their stories of overcoming adversity, countless individuals, including celebrities and everyday people, have contributed to a narrative of resilience and possibility. This campaign has not only raised awareness about the challenges LGBTQ youth face but has also inspired many to become advocates for change in their own communities.

Conclusion

In conclusion, inspiring the next generation of activists through storytelling is a vital aspect of Alec Butler's legacy. By embracing the power of narratives, activists can foster empathy, challenge dominant discourses, and empower individuals to embrace their identities. While there are challenges associated with storytelling, the potential for connection and inspiration far outweighs the risks. As Alec continues to share their story and encourage others to do the same, the ripple effects of these narratives will undoubtedly shape the future of the LGBTQ movement, paving the way for a more inclusive and equitable society.

Reflecting on personal growth and achievements

Overcoming personal challenges and setbacks

Throughout Alec Butler's journey as an LGBTQ activist and artist, the path was often fraught with personal challenges and setbacks that tested their resilience and commitment to the cause. These challenges were not merely obstacles; they were profound learning experiences that shaped Alec's identity and activism.

One significant challenge arose from the intersection of their artistic ambitions and societal expectations. As a Two-Spirit individual, Alec faced the dual pressures of conforming to mainstream artistic standards while also honoring their Indigenous heritage. The theory of intersectionality, as proposed by Kimberlé Crenshaw, highlights how overlapping identities can create unique experiences of discrimination and privilege. In Alec's case, the intersection of their LGBTQ identity and Indigenous background meant that they often felt marginalized within both the LGBTQ community and their Indigenous community. This dual marginalization led to feelings of isolation, but it also fueled a determination to carve out a space for themselves and others who felt similarly excluded.

Alec's early artistic endeavors were met with skepticism from some quarters. Critics would often question the validity of their work, arguing that it was too avant-garde or too focused on political themes. This criticism was disheartening, especially during formative years when validation from peers and mentors is crucial. Alec recalls a pivotal moment during a gallery showing when a prominent art critic dismissed their work as "not real art." This incident, while painful, became a catalyst for growth. Instead of retreating into self-doubt, Alec channeled this setback into motivation. They began to engage deeply with the history of LGBTQ art and the ways in which marginalized voices have historically been silenced. This research not only informed their artistic practice but also solidified their resolve to advocate for greater representation of LGBTQ artists in mainstream art spaces.

In addition to external challenges, Alec grappled with internal struggles related to mental health. The pressure to succeed as a public figure and activist often led to anxiety and moments of self-doubt. Mental health within the LGBTQ community is a critical issue, as studies indicate that LGBTQ individuals are at a higher risk for mental health challenges due to societal stigma and discrimination. Alec's experience mirrors this reality; they often felt the weight of expectations from both the LGBTQ community and the broader society.

To combat these challenges, Alec sought support through therapy and community networks. They found solace in sharing their experiences with other LGBTQ individuals who faced similar struggles. This sense of community became a vital source of strength, illustrating the importance of peer support in overcoming personal challenges. Research has shown that social support can significantly mitigate the effects of stress and anxiety, particularly for marginalized individuals.

Alec's journey also involved confronting the pervasive discrimination within society. One notable experience occurred during a public speaking engagement where they were met with hecklers who shouted homophobic slurs. In that moment, Alec faced a choice: to allow the negativity to silence them or to rise above it. They chose the latter, using the incident as a teaching moment. Alec addressed the hecklers directly, transforming the hostile environment into an opportunity for dialogue about acceptance and understanding. This experience reinforced their belief in the power of resilience and the importance of standing firm in one's identity, even in the face of adversity.

Moreover, setbacks in advocacy work presented their own challenges. For instance, when organizing a protest for LGBTQ rights, Alec encountered logistical issues that threatened to derail the event. Permits were delayed, and funding fell short. Instead of succumbing to frustration, Alec rallied their community, emphasizing the collective power of grassroots activism. They initiated a crowdfunding campaign that not only secured the necessary funds but also strengthened community bonds. This experience underscored the idea that setbacks can serve as springboards for innovation and collaboration.

In reflecting on these personal challenges, Alec emphasizes the importance of resilience. Resilience is not merely the ability to bounce back from adversity; it is the capacity to adapt and grow stronger in the face of challenges. Psychological theories of resilience suggest that individuals who embrace a growth mindset—believing that abilities can be developed through dedication and hard work—are more likely to overcome setbacks. Alec embodies this mindset, using each challenge as an opportunity for personal and collective growth.

Ultimately, Alec Butler's journey is a testament to the power of perseverance. By confronting personal challenges head-on and transforming setbacks into opportunities for growth, they have not only shaped their own identity but have also inspired countless others in the LGBTQ community. Their story serves as a reminder that while the road to activism is often fraught with difficulties, it is through these experiences that true change is forged.

In conclusion, overcoming personal challenges and setbacks is an integral part of Alec's narrative. Each obstacle faced has contributed to their development as an artist and activist, illustrating the profound interplay between personal experiences and broader social movements. As Alec continues to inspire future generations of LGBTQ activists, their journey underscores the importance of resilience, community support, and the unwavering pursuit of equality.

Celebrating milestones and victories in the fight for LGBTQ rights

The journey toward equality for LGBTQ individuals has been marked by numerous milestones that reflect the resilience, courage, and determination of activists like Alec Butler. Celebrating these victories not only acknowledges the progress made but also serves as a reminder of the ongoing struggles faced by the community. Each milestone is a testament to the power of advocacy and the importance of visibility in the fight for rights and recognition.

One of the most significant milestones in LGBTQ history is the decriminalization of homosexuality in Canada, which occurred in 1969. This landmark decision was a direct result of years of activism, public pressure, and changing societal attitudes. The Criminal Code of Canada was amended to decriminalize consensual same-sex relationships, marking a pivotal shift in the legal landscape for LGBTQ individuals. This victory laid the groundwork for future advancements in rights and protections, demonstrating the effectiveness of grassroots activism and the importance of legal reform.

The 1980s and 1990s saw the emergence of AIDS activism, which galvanized the LGBTQ community and brought national attention to the crisis. Organizations like ACT UP (AIDS Coalition to Unleash Power) and the Canadian AIDS Society played crucial roles in advocating for research funding, treatment access, and anti-discrimination policies. The activism surrounding AIDS not only highlighted the urgent need for healthcare equity but also fostered a sense of solidarity within the community. Events such as the annual AIDS Walks and the International AIDS Conference became platforms for raising awareness and celebrating the lives of those lost to the epidemic, transforming grief into a powerful call for change.

In 2005, Canada made history by becoming the fourth country in the world to legalize same-sex marriage. This monumental achievement was the result of tireless advocacy from LGBTQ organizations, legal battles, and public support. The legalization of same-sex marriage represented not only a legal victory but also a cultural shift that recognized the validity of same-sex relationships. Celebrating this milestone involved not only the joyous weddings that followed but also the acknowledgment of the struggles faced by couples who fought for their right to marry. The emotional weight of this victory was palpable, as it symbolized acceptance and equality in the eyes of the law.

Another critical victory was the implementation of the Canadian Human Rights Act amendment in 2017, which added gender identity and expression as prohibited grounds for discrimination. This legislative change was a direct response to the advocacy efforts of transgender individuals and their allies, who highlighted the systemic discrimination faced by the community. Celebrating this victory involved recognizing the importance of intersectionality within the LGBTQ movement, as it underscored the need for inclusive policies that protect all members of the community.

In addition to these legal milestones, cultural victories have also played a significant role in advancing LGBTQ rights. The representation of LGBTQ individuals in media, arts, and politics has evolved dramatically over the years. Celebrating these cultural milestones involves recognizing the contributions of LGBTQ artists, writers, and public figures who have used their platforms to advocate for change. The rise of LGBTQ characters in television and film, as well as the growing visibility of LGBTQ athletes in sports, reflects a broader acceptance and celebration of diverse identities.

Moreover, the annual Pride celebrations that take place across Canada serve as both a celebration of victories and a reminder of the ongoing struggles. Pride parades, festivals, and events are not only opportunities for LGBTQ individuals to celebrate their identities but also serve as platforms for activism and advocacy. They remind the community of the history of resistance against oppression and the importance of continuing the fight for equality.   Celebrating Pride involves honoring the legacy of activists who paved the way, while also acknowledging the work that still needs to be done to ensure that all individuals can live freely and authentically.

As Alec Butler reflects on these milestones and victories, it is essential to celebrate not only the achievements but also the individuals and communities that made them possible.   Each victory is a building block in the ongoing fight for LGBTQ rights, serving as a reminder of the power of collective action and the importance of perseverance.   The journey is far from over, but celebrating these milestones provides hope and inspiration for future generations of activists.

In conclusion, celebrating milestones and victories in the fight for LGBTQ rights is a crucial aspect of acknowledging the progress made and the work that lies ahead. Each victory, whether legal, cultural, or personal, contributes to the larger narrative of resilience and determination within the LGBTQ community. As we continue to advocate for equality and justice, it is vital to honor these milestones as symbols of hope, progress, and the enduring spirit of activism.

Finding balance between personal and activist identities

In the journey of activism, especially within marginalized communities, the interplay between personal identity and activist identity can often become a delicate balancing act. For Alec Butler, this challenge was not merely a theoretical consideration but a lived experience that required constant negotiation and reflection. The struggle to maintain this balance is underscored by the concept of *intersectionality*, as coined by Kimberlé Crenshaw, which posits that individuals experience overlapping and interdependent systems of discrimination or disadvantage.   This framework is particularly relevant when discussing the identities of LGBTQ activists who also navigate the complexities of race, gender, and cultural heritage.

Theoretical Framework

To understand the balance between personal and activist identities, one must first recognize the multifaceted nature of identity itself. Identity can be viewed through the lens of *social identity theory*, which suggests that a person's self-concept is derived from perceived membership in social groups. For Alec, being Two-Spirit and an

LGBTQ activist was not just an aspect of their identity; it was the lens through which they viewed the world and engaged with it. This duality often led to a tension between personal needs and the demands of activism.

$$\text{Self-Concept} = \text{Personal Identity} + \text{Social Identity}$$

This equation highlights that an individual's self-concept is a combination of who they are personally and how they are perceived socially. For activists like Alec, the challenge lies in ensuring that their personal identity is not overshadowed by the weight of their activist responsibilities.

Challenges Faced

One of the primary challenges in balancing these identities is the risk of burnout. Activism can be an all-consuming endeavor, often requiring individuals to prioritize collective goals over personal well-being. Alec faced this challenge firsthand, frequently finding themselves overwhelmed by the emotional toll of advocating for change while simultaneously navigating their personal struggles with identity and acceptance.

The phenomenon of *activist burnout* can be described as a state of emotional, physical, and mental exhaustion caused by prolonged and intense involvement in stressful situations. According to research by *Maslach and Leiter*, burnout can manifest in three dimensions: emotional exhaustion, depersonalization, and a reduced sense of personal accomplishment. For activists, this can lead to feelings of inadequacy and disillusionment, which can further complicate their personal lives.

Strategies for Balance

To combat burnout and find a sustainable balance, Alec employed several strategies:

1. **Setting Boundaries:** Alec learned the importance of setting clear boundaries between their activist work and personal life. This involved designating specific times for activism and ensuring that personal time was respected and prioritized.

2. **Self-Care Practices:** Engaging in self-care became a crucial aspect of Alec's routine. This included activities such as meditation, exercise, and spending time with supportive friends and family, all of which provided necessary respite from the demands of activism.

3. **Community Support:** Building a supportive network of fellow activists allowed Alec to share experiences and seek advice on managing the duality of their identity. This community became a safe space for discussing struggles and celebrating victories, reinforcing the idea that they were not alone in their journey.

4. **Reflective Practices:** Regularly engaging in reflective practices, such as journaling or therapy, helped Alec to process their experiences and emotions. This allowed for a deeper understanding of their motivations and the necessity of maintaining personal authenticity amidst activism.

Examples of Balance in Action

Alec's participation in various LGBTQ events serves as a testament to their commitment to both personal and activist identities. For instance, during Pride Month, Alec not only participated in marches and advocacy meetings but also took time to engage in personal celebrations of their identity, such as attending community potlucks and artistic showcases. These moments of joy and connection helped to reinforce their sense of self and provided a counterbalance to the often heavy emotional labor of activism.

Moreover, Alec's artistic expressions became a powerful tool for merging their personal and activist identities. By creating performances that reflected their experiences as a Two-Spirit individual, Alec was able to share their story with a broader audience while simultaneously honoring their roots. This approach not only provided a cathartic outlet for personal experiences but also served to educate others about the complexities of LGBTQ identities, thereby fostering greater understanding and empathy.

Conclusion

The journey of balancing personal and activist identities is fraught with challenges, yet it is also rich with opportunities for growth and understanding. For Alec Butler, embracing this duality has been essential not only for personal well-being but also for the effectiveness of their activism. As they continue to navigate this intricate landscape, Alec serves as a reminder that authenticity and self-care are paramount in the fight for equality and justice. By prioritizing their personal identity alongside their activist endeavors, Alec not only strengthens their own resolve but also inspires others to embrace the fullness of their identities in the pursuit of change.

In conclusion, the balance between personal and activist identities is a dynamic process that requires ongoing reflection and adaptation. By acknowledging the complexities of their identities and employing strategies to maintain this balance, activists like Alec can continue to advocate for change while nurturing their own well-being and sense of self.

Continuing to learn and evolve as an activist and artist

As Alec Butler navigated the complex landscape of activism and artistry, the journey of continual learning and evolution became a cornerstone of their identity. This process was not merely a passive experience; it was an active engagement with the world, characterized by reflection, adaptation, and growth.

Theoretical Framework

The journey of personal and professional development can be understood through various theoretical lenses. One such framework is Kolb's Experiential Learning Theory, which posits that learning is a process whereby knowledge is created through the transformation of experience. The model consists of four stages: concrete experience, reflective observation, abstract conceptualization, and active experimentation. For Alec, each performance, protest, and public engagement was a concrete experience that prompted reflection on their impact, leading to new insights and strategies for future activism.

The equation that embodies this cycle can be expressed as:

$$L = (E + R) \to A$$

where L represents learning, E is experience, R is reflection, and A is action. This equation illustrates how Alec's experiences in activism and art led to reflective insights, which in turn informed their subsequent actions.

Challenges Faced

Despite the commitment to growth, the path was not devoid of challenges. One significant issue was the intersectionality of identities within the LGBTQ community. Alec recognized that their journey was shaped not only by their identity as a Two-Spirit individual but also by the broader socio-political context that affected various marginalized groups. This complexity often required a nuanced understanding of different perspectives, which could be overwhelming.

For instance, during a public speaking engagement addressing the needs of LGBTQ youth, Alec encountered pushback from some community members who felt their experiences were being overshadowed by the focus on Two-Spirit identities. This moment served as a crucial learning experience, highlighting the importance of inclusive dialogue. Alec learned to actively listen, adapt their messaging, and ensure that all voices were represented, thereby fostering a more inclusive environment.

Examples of Evolution

Alec's evolution as an activist and artist is exemplified through their engagement with new mediums and platforms. Initially rooted in performance art, they began exploring digital media as a means of reaching a wider audience. This transition was not merely a shift in medium but also a significant expansion of their activist toolkit. For example, Alec launched a series of web-based workshops aimed at empowering LGBTQ youth to express their identities through digital storytelling. This initiative not only provided a platform for self-expression but also created a community of support among participants.

Moreover, Alec's collaboration with Indigenous artists enriched their understanding of cultural representation. By participating in art collectives and community projects, they learned to navigate the delicate balance between honoring traditional practices and innovating new forms of expression. This experience reinforced the idea that evolution as an artist requires a willingness to learn from others and to adapt one's approach in response to feedback and changing contexts.

Personal Reflection and Growth

Alec's commitment to personal growth was also evident in their reflective practices. Journaling became a vital tool for processing experiences and emotions. Through writing, Alec could articulate their thoughts on the challenges faced within the activism sphere, such as burnout and the emotional toll of confronting systemic discrimination. This practice not only provided clarity but also served as a source of inspiration for their artistic work.

In one poignant entry, Alec reflected on a particularly challenging protest against anti-LGBTQ legislation. They wrote about the mixed emotions of anger, hope, and solidarity experienced during the event. This reflection later inspired a powerful performance piece that captured the essence of resilience within the LGBTQ community, demonstrating how personal experiences could be transformed into art that resonates with others.

Conclusion

The journey of continuing to learn and evolve as an activist and artist is an ongoing process for Alec Butler. By embracing the complexities of their identity, engaging with diverse perspectives, and reflecting on their experiences, they have cultivated a dynamic approach to activism and artistry. This evolution not only enhances their personal growth but also amplifies the impact of their work within the LGBTQ community and beyond. As Alec continues to navigate the intersection of art and activism, their commitment to learning will undoubtedly inspire others to embark on their own journeys of growth and transformation.

Conclusion

Alec Butler's impact on the LGBTQ movement

The lasting legacy of their activism and advocacy

Alec Butler's activism and advocacy have left an indelible mark on the landscape of LGBTQ rights in Canada, shaping not only the present but also the future of the movement. Their journey, characterized by a relentless pursuit of equality and justice, has set a precedent for both current and future activists. The legacy of Alec's work can be understood through several key lenses: policy change, community empowerment, visibility, and cultural transformation.

Policy Change

One of the most significant aspects of Alec's legacy is their influence on policy reform. Through strategic advocacy, Alec played a pivotal role in the development and implementation of policies that protect LGBTQ rights at both provincial and national levels. For instance, their involvement in campaigns for the inclusion of sexual orientation and gender identity in anti-discrimination laws has had far-reaching implications. According to the *Canadian Charter of Rights and Freedoms*, Section 15 guarantees equality rights, which Alec helped to expand to encompass sexual minorities. This legal framework has empowered countless individuals to seek justice against discrimination, thereby creating a more inclusive society.

Community Empowerment

Alec's commitment to empowering marginalized voices within the LGBTQ community is another cornerstone of their legacy. By fostering grassroots organizations and initiatives, they created platforms for individuals to share their stories and experiences. Programs such as *Youth Speak Out* have provided safe spaces for LGBTQ youth to express themselves, fostering a sense of belonging and community. Alec's belief in the importance of mentorship is evident in their dedication to supporting emerging activists, ensuring that the next generation is equipped with the tools and knowledge to continue the fight for equality.

Visibility

Visibility is a powerful tool in the struggle for rights and recognition. Alec's work has significantly contributed to the visibility of LGBTQ individuals, particularly those who identify as Two-Spirit. By challenging stereotypes and advocating for representation in media and the arts, Alec has helped to normalize diverse identities within the broader cultural narrative. The impact of this visibility is profound; studies show that increased representation in media leads to greater acceptance and understanding in society. For example, Alec's artistic performances, which often highlight the experiences of marginalized communities, have not only captivated audiences but have also sparked important conversations about identity and inclusion.

Cultural Transformation

Alec's advocacy extends beyond legal and policy frameworks; it encompasses a cultural transformation that challenges societal norms and prejudices. Through their performances and public engagements, Alec has confronted homophobia and transphobia head-on, using art as a vehicle for social change. This cultural activism is vital in dismantling harmful stereotypes and fostering empathy among diverse audiences. By engaging with various cultural communities, Alec has promoted intersectionality within the LGBTQ movement, emphasizing the importance of understanding how different identities intersect and impact individuals' experiences.

Theoretical Frameworks

To contextualize Alec's legacy within broader theoretical frameworks, we can draw upon the concepts of *intersectionality* and *social justice*. Intersectionality, as articulated by scholars like Kimberlé Crenshaw, emphasizes the interconnected nature of social categorizations such as race, class, and gender. Alec's work exemplifies this theory by advocating for the rights of Two-Spirit individuals and other marginalized groups within the LGBTQ community. Furthermore, the principles of social justice, which call for equitable distribution of resources and opportunities, resonate deeply with Alec's advocacy efforts. They have championed policies that address systemic inequalities, ensuring that all individuals, regardless of their sexual orientation or gender identity, have access to the same rights and protections.

Conclusion

In conclusion, Alec Butler's lasting legacy is multifaceted, encompassing significant advancements in policy, community empowerment, visibility, and cultural transformation. Their unwavering commitment to justice and equality has not only shaped the landscape of LGBTQ rights in Canada but has also inspired countless individuals to embrace their identities and advocate for change. As the movement continues to evolve, Alec's contributions serve as a guiding light, reminding us of the power of activism and the importance of unfiltered voices in the ongoing struggle for equality. The impact of their work will be felt for generations to come, as new activists build upon the foundation laid by pioneers like Alec Butler.

The significance of their work in the Canadian LGBTQ community

The impact of Alec Butler's activism within the Canadian LGBTQ community cannot be overstated. Their efforts have not only contributed to the visibility and rights of LGBTQ individuals but have also fostered a culture of acceptance and understanding that resonates throughout Canadian society. This section explores the significance of their work, emphasizing the theoretical frameworks, the problems they addressed, and the examples that illustrate their profound influence.

Theoretical Frameworks

To understand the significance of Alec Butler's contributions, we can draw upon several key theoretical frameworks that underpin LGBTQ activism. One such framework is Queer Theory, which challenges the binary understanding of gender and sexuality. Butler's advocacy for Two-Spirit identities exemplifies this theoretical approach by highlighting the fluidity of gender and the importance of intersectionality within the LGBTQ movement.

Another relevant framework is Social Movement Theory, which examines how collective action can lead to social change. Butler's strategic involvement in protests and demonstrations exemplifies this theory, as they mobilized communities to challenge systemic discrimination and advocate for policy changes. The interplay between these theories elucidates the multifaceted nature of Butler's activism and its significance in shaping the Canadian LGBTQ landscape.

Addressing Systemic Issues

One of the most pressing problems that Butler confronted was the systemic discrimination faced by LGBTQ individuals in Canada. Despite significant advancements in legal rights, many LGBTQ individuals still experience discrimination in various sectors, including employment, healthcare, and housing. Butler's work in exposing these injustices was crucial in raising awareness and advocating for comprehensive anti-discrimination policies.

For instance, Butler's involvement in the 2017 campaign for the repeal of discriminatory policies within the Canadian Armed Forces highlighted the ongoing issues of homophobia and transphobia in institutions that were supposed to protect citizens. By bringing these issues to light, Butler not only challenged the status quo but also inspired a new generation of activists to continue the fight for equality.

Examples of Impact

Alec Butler's significance can be illustrated through several key initiatives and accomplishments that have left a lasting mark on the Canadian LGBTQ community.

- ♦ **The Creation of Safe Spaces:** Butler was instrumental in establishing safe spaces for LGBTQ youth, where they could express their identities without fear of judgment or discrimination. This initiative not only provided immediate support but also fostered a sense of community and belonging among marginalized youth.

- ♦ **Advocacy for Two-Spirit Representation:** Butler's efforts to elevate Two-Spirit voices within the LGBTQ movement have been vital in challenging the marginalization of Indigenous LGBTQ individuals. By collaborating with Indigenous activists, Butler has helped to create a more inclusive movement that recognizes the diverse experiences within the LGBTQ community.

- ♦ **Media Engagement:** Through their appearances on various media platforms, Butler has effectively utilized the power of storytelling to humanize LGBTQ issues. By sharing personal experiences and insights, they have educated the public and fostered empathy, thereby reducing stigma and promoting acceptance.

Legacy and Continuing Influence

The significance of Alec Butler's work extends beyond immediate activism; it has laid the groundwork for future generations of LGBTQ activists. Their mentorship of emerging voices within the community ensures that the fight for equality continues to evolve and adapt to new challenges.

Moreover, Butler's emphasis on intersectionality has encouraged a more holistic approach to LGBTQ advocacy, where the unique experiences of individuals from diverse backgrounds are acknowledged and addressed. This shift has profound implications for the Canadian LGBTQ community, as it fosters a more inclusive and united front in the fight for rights and recognition.

In conclusion, Alec Butler's contributions to the Canadian LGBTQ community are significant not only for their immediate impact but also for the enduring legacy they have created. By challenging systemic discrimination, advocating for marginalized voices, and fostering a culture of acceptance, Butler has played a pivotal role in shaping the landscape of LGBTQ rights in Canada. Their work serves as a reminder of the importance of activism in creating a more equitable society, inspiring countless individuals to embrace their identities and join the ongoing fight for equality.

Inspiring others to embrace their identities and fight for equality

Alec Butler's journey is not just a personal narrative; it is a beacon for countless individuals grappling with their own identities. Through their activism, Alec has demonstrated that embracing one's true self is not merely an act of personal liberation but a powerful catalyst for social change. This section explores how Alec's work has inspired others to embrace their identities and engage in the fight for equality, drawing on relevant theories, challenges faced by LGBTQ individuals, and concrete examples of impact.

Theoretical Framework: Identity and Empowerment

At the core of Alec's influence is the concept of identity empowerment, which posits that individuals who embrace their identities are better equipped to advocate for themselves and others. According to *Social Identity Theory* (Tajfel & Turner, 1979), individuals derive a sense of self from their group memberships, which can significantly impact their self-esteem and behavior. For LGBTQ individuals, embracing their identity can lead to increased resilience against societal discrimination and the courage to advocate for change.

Alec's advocacy work highlights the intersection of identity and activism. By publicly embracing their Two-Spirit identity, Alec has not only validated their own experiences but has also encouraged others to find strength in their identities. This is particularly crucial in a society where LGBTQ individuals often face stigma and marginalization.

Challenges Faced by LGBTQ Individuals

Despite the progress made in LGBTQ rights, many individuals still face significant barriers that can hinder their ability to embrace their identities. These challenges include:

+ **Internalized Homophobia:** Many LGBTQ individuals struggle with self-acceptance due to societal stigma. This internal conflict can lead to mental health issues, including anxiety and depression.

+ **Discrimination and Violence:** The fear of discrimination or violence can prevent individuals from expressing their identities openly. This is especially true for marginalized subgroups within the LGBTQ community, such as transgender and Two-Spirit individuals.

+ **Lack of Representation:** A pervasive lack of representation in media and leadership roles can lead to feelings of invisibility among LGBTQ individuals, making it difficult for them to envision a future where they can be their authentic selves.

Alec's work addresses these challenges head-on, providing a counter-narrative that encourages individuals to embrace their identities despite societal pressures.

Concrete Examples of Impact

One of the most profound ways Alec has inspired others is through their public speaking engagements. By sharing their story of self-discovery and activism, Alec has connected with diverse audiences, empowering individuals to embrace their identities. For instance, during a keynote speech at the *Pride in the Military* conference, Alec shared their experiences as a Two-Spirit individual navigating the complexities of military life. Their candidness resonated with many attendees, prompting several to publicly identify as LGBTQ for the first time.

In addition to public speaking, Alec has utilized social media as a platform for advocacy. Posts highlighting their journey, along with supportive messages for LGBTQ youth, have garnered significant attention, creating a sense of community among followers. For example, a viral post featuring Alec's artwork and a message of self-acceptance led to an outpouring of responses from individuals sharing their own stories of coming out and embracing their identities.

Moreover, Alec's collaboration with LGBTQ organizations has resulted in initiatives aimed at fostering self-acceptance among youth. One such initiative, the *Embrace Your Identity* workshop series, provides a safe space for LGBTQ youth to explore their identities through creative expression. Participants engage in art, writing, and discussion, allowing them to connect with others who share similar experiences. Feedback from participants has highlighted the transformative impact of these workshops, with many expressing newfound confidence in their identities.

The Ripple Effect of Inspiration

The impact of Alec's work extends beyond individual stories; it creates a ripple effect throughout the community. As more individuals embrace their identities, they become advocates for change, contributing to a broader movement for equality. This phenomenon is supported by the *Collective Identity Theory*, which suggests that shared experiences among marginalized groups can foster a sense of solidarity and collective action (Polletta & Jasper, 2001).

Alec's influence can be seen in the growing number of LGBTQ individuals who are stepping into leadership roles within their communities. By sharing their stories and advocating for equality, these individuals are not only changing their own lives but also inspiring others to do the same. This collective movement is essential for dismantling systemic barriers and achieving lasting change.

Conclusion: The Power of Authenticity

Alec Butler's journey exemplifies the power of authenticity in inspiring others to embrace their identities and fight for equality. By sharing their story and advocating for change, Alec has illuminated the path for countless individuals navigating their own journeys of self-discovery. The challenges faced by LGBTQ individuals are significant, but through empowerment, representation, and community engagement, Alec has proven that embracing one's identity can be a powerful force for change. As more individuals find the courage to be their authentic selves, the collective fight for equality grows stronger, paving the way for a more inclusive and just society.

Bibliography

[1] Tajfel, H., & Turner, J. C. (1979). An integrative theory of intergroup conflict. In *The Social Psychology of Intergroup Relations* (pp. 33-47). Brooks/Cole.

[2] Polletta, F., & Jasper, J. M. (2001). Collective identity and social movements. *The Annual Review of Sociology, 27*(1), 283-305.

The importance of unfiltered voices in the LGBTQ movement

The LGBTQ movement has historically thrived on the strength of its diverse voices, each contributing a unique perspective that reflects the complexity of individual experiences within the community. Unfiltered voices are essential in this context, as they challenge dominant narratives, highlight injustices, and foster a sense of belonging among marginalized individuals. The significance of these voices can be analyzed through several theoretical frameworks, including intersectionality, representation theory, and the social model of disability.

Intersectionality

Intersectionality, a term coined by Kimberlé Crenshaw, emphasizes the interconnectedness of various social identities, including race, gender, sexual orientation, and class. This framework illustrates how individuals experience oppression differently based on their unique social positions. In the LGBTQ movement, unfiltered voices allow for the representation of these intersections, ensuring that the experiences of, for example, a Two-Spirit Indigenous person are not overshadowed by the narratives of more privileged LGBTQ individuals.

For instance, the advocacy of Two-Spirit activists has brought to light the specific challenges faced by Indigenous LGBTQ individuals, including cultural erasure and systemic discrimination. By amplifying these unfiltered voices, the movement can address the multifaceted nature of oppression and advocate for policies that are inclusive of all identities.

$$O = f(I_1, I_2, I_3, \ldots, I_n) \tag{25}$$

Where O is the overall oppression experienced by an individual, and I_n represents the various intersecting identities that contribute to that experience.

Representation Theory

Representation theory posits that the visibility of diverse identities in media and public discourse is crucial for fostering acceptance and understanding. Unfiltered voices in the LGBTQ movement challenge stereotypes and provide authentic portrayals of LGBTQ lives, countering the often narrow and sensationalized depictions found in mainstream media.

For example, the rise of social media platforms has allowed LGBTQ individuals to share their stories in their own words, bypassing traditional gatekeepers. This democratization of voice has led to a richer tapestry of narratives, showcasing the diversity of experiences within the community. Hashtags such as #TransIsBeautiful and #BlackAndQueer have emerged, creating spaces for dialogue and solidarity among marginalized groups.

The Social Model of Disability

The social model of disability argues that disability is not an inherent trait but rather a result of societal barriers. This perspective can be applied to the LGBTQ movement, where unfiltered voices highlight the societal constructs that contribute to discrimination and exclusion.

For instance, the activism of disabled LGBTQ individuals, such as the work of Alice Wong and her organization, the Disability Visibility Project, underscores the importance of including disability narratives within the broader LGBTQ discourse. By sharing their experiences, these activists reveal how societal attitudes and infrastructures create barriers to equality, advocating for a more inclusive movement that recognizes the rights of all individuals, regardless of ability.

Challenges to Unfiltered Voices

Despite the importance of unfiltered voices, challenges remain. Marginalized individuals often face backlash for speaking out, including threats, harassment, and silencing tactics. The phenomenon of "cancel culture" can also stifle dissenting opinions within the LGBTQ community, leading to a homogenization of voices that undermines the very diversity the movement seeks to promote.

Moreover, the intersection of race and sexuality can complicate the visibility of voices within the LGBTQ movement. For example, Black LGBTQ activists often find their narratives overshadowed by the dominant white LGBTQ discourse. This marginalization can perpetuate a cycle of invisibility, where unfiltered voices are not only silenced but also erased from the historical record.

Examples of Impact

Several examples illustrate the transformative power of unfiltered voices in the LGBTQ movement. The Stonewall Riots of 1969, often cited as the catalyst for the modern LGBTQ rights movement, were driven by the raw and unfiltered expressions of anger and frustration from marginalized individuals, particularly transgender women of color like Marsha P. Johnson and Sylvia Rivera. Their voices were instrumental in shaping the movement's direction, emphasizing the need for radical change.

More recently, the #MeToo movement has highlighted the importance of unfiltered voices in addressing sexual violence within the LGBTQ community. Activists like Tarana Burke and Alyssa Milano have shown that sharing personal stories can empower others to come forward, fostering solidarity and collective action against systemic abuse.

Conclusion

In conclusion, unfiltered voices are vital to the LGBTQ movement as they enrich the discourse, challenge existing power structures, and foster a sense of community among diverse identities. By embracing these voices, the movement can ensure that all individuals are represented, valued, and empowered to advocate for their rights. The ongoing struggle for equality necessitates the amplification of unfiltered voices, as they are the heartbeat of a movement that seeks to create a world where everyone can live authentically and without fear. The journey toward liberation is not just about achieving rights; it is about creating a space where every voice is heard, respected, and celebrated.

Index

Milton Keynes UK
Ingram Content Group UK Ltd.
UKHW020318021124
450424UK00013B/1322